EMPATHIC
BRIEF
PSYCHOTHERAPY

EMPATHIC
BRIEF
PSYCHOTHERAPY

❖ ❖ ❖

BARBARA B. SERUYA, PH.D.

JASON ARONSON INC.
Northvale, New Jersey
London

This book was set in 11 pt. Weiss by Alpha Graphics of Pittsfield, New Hampshire, and printed and bound by Book-mart Press of North Bergen, New Jersey.

Library of Congress Cataloging-in-Publication Data
Seruya, Barbara B.
    Empathic brief psychotherapy / by Barbara B. Seruya.
        p.   cm.
    Includes bibliographical references and index.
    ISBN 0-7657-0067-0 (alk. paper)
    1. Self psychology. 2. Brief psychotherapy. 3. Empathy.
I. Title.
[DNLM: 1. Psychotherapy, Brief. 2. Empathy. WM 420.5.P5 S489e
1997]
RC489.S43S47 1997
616.89'14—dc21
DNLM/DLC
for Library of Congress   97-638

Printed in the United States of America on acid-free paper. Jason Aronson Inc. offers books and cassettes. For information and catalog write to Jason Aronson Inc., 230 Livingston Street, Northvale, New Jersey 07647. Or visit our website: http://www.aronson.com

DEDICATION

I wish to dedicate this book to all those who inspired and supported this effort. It would not have been possible at all without the affirming experience, invaluable emotional support, and intellectual rigor that my husband, Carlton E. Wynter, Jr., Ph.D., brought to the project. It would not have been as proud an effort without the support of my first selfobject and father, Benjamin Seruya.

I would like to express my gratitude for the support and analytic dialogues engaged in with Jane Wilkins, Ph.D. I also want to acknowledge the long hours of research contributed to this effort by my assistant, Rebecca Chisman. Finally, I want to thank all my clients whose lives illuminated the therapy experience for me.

❖ CONTENTS ❖

1 Introduction   1
Crisis in Our Health Care System   2
The Impact of Managed Care on the Practice of Psychotherapy   3
What is Brief Psychotherapy?   3
Principles of Self Psychology Used in Empathic Brief Psychotherapy   8

2 An Introduction to Self Psychology   11
Empathy   12
Narcissism   13
The Influence of Infant Research on Self Psychology   13
The Self in Self Psychology   15
Self Psychological Orientation to Therapy   22

3 An Introduction to the Brief Psychotherapies   27
Defining Brief Therapy   27
Cognitive-Behavioral Therapy   40
Integrating Cognitive-Behavioral Elements with Self Psychology   44

4 Derivation of the Current Model   49
Newer Conceptual Metaphors for Brief Psychotherapy   49
Earlier Attempts to Adapt Self Psychology to Shorter-Term Therapy   55
Key Aspects of the Empathic Brief Psychotherapy Model   58

Cognitive-Behavioral Integration Within a Self Psychology Model   61
Informal Case Presentation   62

5 Empathic Brief Psychotherapy with Individuals   65
Beginning Empathic Short-Term Therapy   65
Case Material from the Beginning Phase of Empathic Brief Therapy   71
Middle and End Phases of Therapy   80
Ending Empathic Brief Treatment   86

6 Therapist and Client Issues with Brief Therapy   95
General Problematic Reactions to the Brief Therapy Experience   95
Aspects of Managed Care that Trigger Therapist
    and Client Reactions   98
Use of Adjuncts to Short-Term Psychotherapy   102

7 Empathic Brief Psychotherapy with Couples   105
Background   105
Couple Breakdown   107
Current Model of Applying Self Psychology to
    Brief Couples Treatment   109
Chronology of Key Features of the Model   111
Case Example: Beginning Couples Therapy   114
Middle Phase of Couples Therapy   122
End Phase of Couples Therapy   126

8 Doing Brief Psychotherapy Under Managed Care   133
An Historical Perspective   135
Guidelines on Working with Managed Care Organizations   136

References   145

Index   153

CHAPTER 1

INTRODUCTION

One of my initial interests in the field of psychology was altered states of consciousness. I am still quite intrigued by this field of study. Put simply, an altered state refers to a state of being in which the individual feels a qualitative shift in his pattern of mental functioning. It can be induced by various physiological, pharmacological, or psychological stimuli. It has occurred to me that the massive changes in the health care field may have thrown us clinicians into an altered state of consciousness.

The way we may need to practice has altered the identity of many mental health professionals. As a result, we now inhabit a different intersubjective space with our patients during the therapy hour. How we experience doing short-term therapy with our patients in the current health care environment feels qualitatively different. Why is brief therapy the battle cry and what has happened to American health care?

Planned, short-term therapy developed largely as a result of the community mental health movement of the 1960s. It was a way to deliver services to a much larger population within an efficient time frame. However, as Bloom (1992) points out, this modality was meant to address the mental health needs of the community and to coexist with time-unlimited therapy rather than replace it. But socioeconomic and political forces and cultural pressures were to bring this newer modality to the fore.

One of the forces may have been a trend in consumer attitudes and values. Consumers perceive themselves as increasingly having less available time, money, and energy. And we all want more value for our money. However, the new attitude of the consumer represents just one part of the story.

CRISIS IN OUR HEALTH CARE SYSTEM

Health care costs are perceived to be one of the major reasons for the explosive change in how health care services are funded and provided. But the issues of access to care and quality of care are also driving the changes in the health care arena even more so than in the 1960s. Yenney (1994) points out that health care spending in the United States rose approximately 4000 percent between 1960 and 1990. She cites Sonnefeld and colleagues (1993) as projecting that spending will rise 70 percent more by the year 2000.

The United States spends more of its gross national product (GNP) on health care than most of its European competitors, creating an international disadvantage for us. In 1993 the federal government spent approximately 17 percent of its overall budget on health care. As a result, various health care programs must compete among themselves for shrinking government dollars. The federal and state governments as well as political parties are each planning an overhaul of the health care system in order to contain costs and improve quality of care and access to care.

The private sector ultimately assumes a large part of the burden of the cost of health care services through its provision of health insurance to employees and their dependents. Yenney (1994) indicates that the per-employee cost of providing mental health care doubled between 1987 and 1992. Therefore, any increase or decrease in health care costs is of great interest to business. Yenney further notes that mental health treatment costs in the United States are more than $65 billion per year. Concurring with other sources, she observes that most of the costs stem from adolescent treatment and substance abuse treatment, especially on the inpatient services.

Businesses have tried to address this rise in health care spending through "cost shifting," which includes increasing employee co-payments, their deductibles, and other out-of-pocket expenses. While mental health practitioners had been anxiously monitoring proposed mental health care reforms by the government, corporate America stepped in and began to institute its own changes. In addition to cost shifting, businesses have engaged managed care organizations, established employee assistance programs, and established their own provider networks to control costs. Now the health care companies are devouring each other and forming mega health corporations. Other contributions to today's health crisis will be noted in a later chapter on managed care.

THE IMPACT OF MANAGED CARE ON THE PRACTICE OF PSYCHOTHERAPY

Some clinicians are embracing the changes and are enthusiastic about managed care and brief therapy. Others are trying to adapt by diversifying their professional roles away from psychotherapy. Some are leaving the therapy field as a result of drastically reduced fees and number of referrals.

Many therapists are attempting to use short-term approaches, perhaps for the first time in their careers. They worry that patients may experience brief treatment as either confronting or just supportive. Patients may then "complete" treatment feeling either not understood or that their underlying dysfunctional patterns were inadequately addressed.

Saakvitne and Abrahamson (1994) refer to the clinician's side of the crisis, and pointedly state, "While everyone cites the economic and social factors that have contributed to the proliferation of managed care, we rarely examine how our own training and practice have contributed to our unreadiness to respond in a systematic and thoughtful way" (p. 181). I hope this book will begin a thoughtful response.

WHAT IS BRIEF PSYCHOTHERAPY?

Brief dynamic therapy or short-term, planned treatment is a form of psychotherapy that customarily lasts from one to twenty-five sessions and the time frame is usually short from beginning of treatment to termination. (Treatment can consist of a few sessions but stretched out over a long period of time. Planned *brief* therapy usually consists of a few sessions conducted in a fairly short span of time. It does not refer to length of time of an individual session.) Currently, the average number of sessions may be dropping to about ten, which approximates the national average (Lowman and Resnick 1994). The sessions are focused on particular issues rather than being open-ended. The patient is an active collaborator in the treatment and the therapist is much more active than in traditional long-term approaches.

Brief treatment offers new challenges to the therapist as well as to the patient. Some therapists have difficulty integrating familiar value systems and long-used treatment approaches with the new time limits and extra-treatment parameters. Many therapists do believe that brief approaches provide symptomatic relief at best. To some therapists, the techniques for doing brief therapy can seem insensitive to the patient, almost surgical and lacking in empathy.

For those therapists who use an empathic, relational, or interpersonal theoretical orientation, the requirement to involve themselves and the patient deeply in the therapy process makes for more intense emotional upheavals. Without further guideposts for doing brief work, dynamic therapists are prone to deviations in technique and countertransference that may undermine the patient's treatment as well as their own psychic equilibrium.

However, there are several advantages to learning and applying brief therapy. For many practitioners who have specialized in long-term treatment, a brief approach adds diversity to their practice. It will probably increase referral sources. The challenge of doing brief therapy can add rigor to the therapeutic process. The time or session limit imposed on the treatment may motivate the patient to get quickly and deeply involved in it. When patients continue to do therapeutic work outside of the sessions they can feel more masterful. Many more people can be helped when treatment lasts a shorter time. Finally, access to brief treatment by a larger target population may culturally reduce the stigma of entering psychotherapy, thereby encouraging more people to seek help.

Most of us working in the field are convinced of the effectiveness of psychotherapy in alleviating symptoms and improving psychological functioning. But solid research to document that effectiveness has been late in coming, relatively scarce, and lacking in consistent findings. The good news from the developing psychotherapy research literature (Howard et al. 1986) is that, in general, psychotherapy works and is considered quite helpful to patients (Shapiro and Shapiro 1982, Smith et al. 1980).

Consumer Reports (1995) conducted a large, in-depth survey on mental health care and therapy effectiveness from 1991 to 1994. This survey complemented the more common controlled efficacy studies that indicate resoundingly that therapy works. Some 4,100 people answered twenty-six questions about the nature of their therapy, including their psychological state at the start of treatment and now, the nature of their problems, the treatment modalities employed, therapist competency, health care coverage, the degree to which therapy helped, the ways in which therapy helped, satisfaction with therapy, and reasons for termination. Seligman (1995) pointed out that while the *Consumer Reports* survey had its limitations, it was very significant in that it surveyed and analyzed how therapy patients "fare under the actual conditions of treatment in the field" (p. 966).

Results showed that clients benefited substantially from therapy. Psychotherapy alone did not differ in effectiveness from psychotherapy combined with medication. No specific modality did better than any other for a specific disorder. The results also suggested that the longer people stayed in therapy the more they improved.

This book does not intend to convert people to doing brief work and to give up their time-unlimited work. Nor does it intend to prove conclusively the worth of brief therapy with various imperfect therapy research studies. Yet it is important to be aware that some therapy research (Taube et al. 1988) suggests that long-term psychotherapy is not typical for most patients, and it may be that 10 percent of patients may be using more than 50 percent of mental health resources. With the probability that over 50 million people may be suffering with a mental or addictive disorder in this country, clearly clinicians need to be able to conduct brief therapy. The following research is cited to provide some measure of comfort and validation regarding the benefits of incorporating this newer modality.

Early research (Butcher and Koss 1978, Malan 1963, Sifneos 1979, Strupp and Hadley 1979) on the outcome of *brief* psychotherapy in particular had suggested that short-term treatment is effective in bringing about change in the area of the focal problem. Consequently this therapy was thought to be successful in modifying a narrow part of the client's personality. Few pretenses were made that short-term treatment could bring about the range and depth of change that long-term analytic work could possibly facilitate. Yet, Hoyt (1985) notes that some early researchers (Bloom 1981, Malan et al. 1975) had found that even a single therapeutic interview could produce benefits in terms of the client's understanding of his focal problem, and his ability to do something about it, in long-term follow-up.

While the findings of meta-analytic studies in particular need to be carefully scrutinized, it is interesting to note that Smith and Glass (1977) conducted a study of time-unlimited therapy that has implications for brief therapy as well. They conducted a meta-analysis of approximately 400 psychotherapy outcome studies covering over 25,000 patients. They found that patients did 75 percent better than their untreated control subjects on therapy outcome measures and that the average length of treatment was seventeen sessions.

In a more recent meta-analysis of psychotherapy studies Howard and colleagues (1986) looked at the relationship between the number of therapy sessions and the percentage of patients who improved. They used data from their own studies and other studies involving 2,400 therapy outpatients covering a period of 30 years of research. The data sampled a range of treatment settings from private practice to community clinics. Therapists came from all of the major mental health professions and were predominantly psychodynamic in orientation. Patient diagnoses were mostly in the neurotic anxiety and depressive categories, while a smaller number of diagnoses were in the borderline and psychotic categories. Outcome criteria included patient self-ratings throughout the course of treatment, researcher ratings of patient improvement from chart material, and therapist ratings of patient improvement at the end of treatment.

The authors found that 48 to 58 percent of patients measurably improved by the eighth session. Approximately 75 percent of patients measurably improved by twenty-six sessions, and 85 percent showed improvement with one year of therapy. Looking at the different diagnostic categories, they found that depressive patients responded soonest (in eight to thirteen sessions) to treatment, followed by the anxious patients, while the borderline and psychotic patients took longer (thirteen to twenty-six sessions) to respond to treatment.

Due to all the pressures cited, many clinicians have been catapulted into doing brief treatment. Often they approach short-term treatment unsystematically and with varying degrees of comfort and success. Yet we are hearing that short-term psychotherapy is an effective therapeutic modality. It needs to be considered as a treatment option when seeing patients in consultation rather than assuming that everyone who enters the office needs longer-term therapy. When we deal with managed care situations that decision may be predetermined.

Short-term psychotherapy as it is conducted in the present cannot address all the mental health issues of our population and replace longer-term therapy, but we must be skilled to provide both. So, where do we turn for an approach that is effective for the client and relatively easily applied by the clinician? The answer may be an approach to which clinicians can adapt their current methods.

My Approach to Short-Term Therapy

Aspects of this treatment approach were originally developed in collaboration with JoAnn Magdoff, Ph.D., a psychoanalytic psychotherapist practicing in New York. We had been applying this short-term treatment approach for several years in individual treatment, couples treatment, and crisis intervention, as well as in conducting supervision.

This therapy model represents an integration of my initial training in cognitive-behavior therapy with a long-standing interest in psychodynamic approaches, specifically self psychology. My clinical attitudes have been affected also by conducting qualitative research in consumer behavior, another professional role of mine. In this other arena one always tries to identify those services and products that consumers need and want.

Some clinicians connect Kohut and self psychology with a treatment approach narrowly geared to those diagnosed with a narcissistic disorder. That is where the approach developed, but it grew to become a general theory of development and treatment. Across the diagnostic categories, clinicians, medical doctors, and clergy more and more encounter people suffering from a constellation of problems, including low self-esteem, defensive grandiosity, depression, and anxiety. They have difficulty regulating their reactions to stress, struggle to pursue their ambitions, feel bored and empty inside, and develop compulsive behaviors (including addictions) and hypochondriacal complaints with consequent problems in interpersonal relationships. We can comprehend these difficulties as caused by underlying disorders of the self, which can be addressed more successfully by self psychologically informed therapy.

I am impressed with the effectiveness of self psychology in providing patients not only symptom relief but also an opportunity for renewed growth. It is exciting and satisfying for the therapist as well to work on the deeper levels to which an empathic stance takes us.

However, all the current treatment approaches are delimited in some fashion by the way they conceptualize goals for therapy, the way they conceptualize pathology, and their mode of intervention. Psychoanalysts tend to focus more on affect and motivation, cognitive therapists focus on thinking, and learning theorists focus on behavior. Considering the very limited time and resources we have in which to do brief therapy, we must try to address the patient's problems as they are manifested in more areas of functioning.

The clinical experience from which this developing model is based comes significantly from many years of working at inner-city hospitals in inpatient and outpatient services, as well from private practice work. Therapy was conducted with clients of varied socioeconomic status, age, racial and ethnic backgrounds, and sexual orientation.

The challenge was to develop a brief treatment method that would benefit the patient, stimulate the therapist, and provide more than just temporary or "Band-Aid" relief to the patient. Therapists typically underestimate how therapeutic the first several sessions are for the patient and therefore find brief treatment unsatisfying. We tend to discount such brief work as consultations, crisis intervention, phone contacts, or the initial work done before a client drops out of time-unlimited treatment. What I and others have learned is that even one contact with a skilled, empathic therapist or consultant can help the client change in small ways that might ultimately have greater ramifications in the client's life.

There may be an added benefit for the client to be treated with this empathic approach. Often the lay public fears that therapists want to fit clients into their schema of what it is to be "normal" or "healthy." This model requires that the therapist view each person's dynamics, strengths, and weaknesses as forming a unique constellation. It is this unique human constellation that must be understood and addressed in each therapy session. As a result prospective clients may find this therapy more attractive and reassuring to them because their uniqueness and specialness will be fostered, not stifled.

PRINCIPLES OF SELF PSYCHOLOGY USED IN EMPATHIC BRIEF PSYCHOTHERAPY

This treatment model attempts to integrate major self psychology concepts and strategies with aspects of cognitive and behavioral techniques into brief individual treatment. Case material is presented to help practitioners begin to think through a humane, psychodynamic approach to short-term treatment. Here are some important elements of this integrated approach.

Creating a nourishing, effective client–therapist relationship is key to this approach. The patient experiences the therapy relationship as providing consistent empathic selfobject interchanges, which initiate the internalization of aliveness, hope, enhanced intrapsychic organization, improved cognitive function and action, and ultimately improved object relatedness.

The selfobject functions that the therapist serves may change during the treatment process. As these functions become identified and internalized in the patient, they form the foundation on which the patient can continue to work to further his own growth.

Self States

In this approach attempts are made to appreciate the multidimensional and often nonlinear ways that human beings experience and behave. States of mind, specifically the patterned ways in which the client experiences his own self, are explored. In line with Kohut (1984) and Lichtenberg and colleagues (1992), I also emphasize the therapist's need to comprehend and assess on an ongoing basis the state of the self of the patient in order to be attuned and optimally responsive to the patient. This presumes that the clinician takes soundings of her self state too in reacting to the patient. When conducting short-term psychotherapy this becomes even more challenging, but it is important to consider.

Lichtenberg and colleagues (1992) define the patient's self state, as used in their assessment of the self, as "an overall affective-cognitive-kinesthetic organization of the self. . . . In each state, the rules that govern motivations, cognition, affects, and behaviors vary predictably" (p. 75). It is to these patterns that the therapist needs to be attuned, and even more important, in brief therapy, to train the patient to be attuned to as well.

Self psychology concepts are applied to enable us to see the underlying dynamics, and begin to address core pathology in a specific sector of the client's personality. Disorders in thinking and behavior are understood more as sequelae of the underlying stresses to the self that then feed back to the affective state. Through empathic work, self functioning can be enhanced, and consequently, distorted thinking and maladaptive behaviors can be modified. Cognitive and behavioral symptoms may also be the simultaneous direct focus of intervention depending on the nature of the client's difficulties.

Hypotheses, that is, interpretations, derived from self psychology concepts are offered to the patient to help understand and explain his or her issues. But this clinical approach attempts to downplay the adherence to only one traditional theory or set of techniques in favor of the use of the curative role of the therapeutic relationship. This approach is supported by many clinicians and researchers. Gustafson (1981, 1984) addresses this specifically in analyzing a forerunner of brief self psychological therapy developed by Balint and colleagues (1972). In his analyses of brief therapy conducted at the Tavistock Clinic for over twenty-five years, Gustafson affirms that the curative factors in conducting brief therapy went beyond interpreting the unconscious focal conflict. Rather, the curative factors had more to do with what the therapist provided the patient in their interactions.

With the application of self psychology to brief treatment, clinicians will be able to think dynamically in doing brief work. Both therapist and patient often experience it as a more humane, yet effective approach. Many clinicians perceive it to be an approach that is flexible enough to assist patients in restoring them to a former level of functioning or to begin the process of structure building. The central tenets of self psychology also offer a more general yet effective way of working with clients in any human service delivery system.

CHAPTER 2

AN INTRODUCTION
TO SELF PSYCHOLOGY

Self psychology is a theory formulated by Heinz Kohut (1971, 1977, 1984) in the early 1970s to explain healthy as well as disturbed psychological development. Its original emphasis was on the treatment of narcissistic disorders. Kohut, a mainstream psychoanalyst, started to reformulate the concepts and methods of psychoanalysis in 1959, partly to address these kinds of disorders. In collaboration with Wolf and others, he ultimately created a psychoanalytic theory and treatment model that emphasized developmental growth as well as the reparation of psychological deficits. In this system, as Baker (1991) indicates, Kohut emphasized "the supraordinate position of the self in motivating behavior" (p. 288). Let's take a look at some of the history and concepts of this analytic approach.

Freud's pioneering method of psychoanalysis proved to be very successful in treating symptom neuroses, especially in comparison to the alternative treatment approaches to mental disorders available in the early 1900s. Treatment of behavior and character disorders, however, was often unsuccessful. Early analysts felt these kinds of patients were unanalyzable.

Many social scientists, including Kohut (1984) and Wolf (1988), believed that Western society had changed since Freud's time, when symptom neuroses were dominant. In the twentieth century we seemed to see more clients affected by alienation and emptiness, perhaps due to the fragmentation of the family and the impoverishment of societal resources that could help sustain people. Chronic neglect by others more often resulted in individual responses of anger and depression and in maladaptive attempts at repair, such as the overstimulation or deadening of oneself.

Kohut was confounded by his efforts to help a whole class of people for whom his training had not fully prepared him. In his attempt to better help such patients as those with narcissistic, behavior, and character disorders, Kohut developed the clinical method of vicarious introspection (a.k.a. empathy) with which to understand his clients and ultimately to treat them. Given the symptom picture presented by such clients, like-minded therapists began to refer to these myriad disorders as disorders of the self.

EMPATHY

Kohut's use of a sustained empathic stance while working with such clients led to his observations and delineation of the selfobject transferences. In his efforts to work through the selfobject transferences, Kohut articulated the concept of the selfobject, the cornerstone of his approach.

Empathy in the therapy relationship is the prime data-gathering tool in psychoanalysis and plays a curative role. Later self psychologists would elaborate that empathy plays an essential and major curative role either directly as a reparative process in itself or through facilitating major exploration and interpretation. The analyst systematically and empathically immerses himself in the subjective world of the patient and does so in a sustained manner throughout treatment. The subjective world of the patient becomes the field of inquiry.

Many self psychologists, including the author, have enlarged the field or changed the balance of foreground (patient) and background (therapist) of the field of inquiry to include how the two subjective worlds of patient and therapist interact or collide.

Certainly many other therapists have worked empathically and have stressed the importance of the self, both within and outside the psychoanalytic school, especially Winnicott and others of the British school of object relations, and Carl Rogers. However, none gave these concepts the central, systematic data gathering and curative roles they have within self psychology.

NARCISSISM

In addition to making the self the overarching focus in personality development and empathy its primary tool, Kohut also reexamined and redefined the role of narcissism. Freud had posited that infants start out selfish, completely self-absorbed, and grandiose—that is, narcissistic. The infant learned to love others (achieve object love) as separate beings only after it mastered various psychosexual developmental tasks. If one continued to be narcissistic as an adult, that was a form of disorder.

Kohut came to believe that self regard and self love were not immaturity or synonymous with narcissism. There was a healthy form of narcissism that was a part of human development, and there was a pathological form. Pathological narcissism was viewed as a result of one's self chronically not being appropriately nurtured. Therefore, there must be separate lines of development for how infants come to love other people and how they come to love and nurture their selves.

Healthy narcissism was now considered an aspect of self-esteem. As Kohut and others fleshed out the clinical theory, it became clearer that the preservation and growth of the person's whole self, rather than the vicissitudes of instincts or state of the person's ego, was the dynamic core of what needed to be addressed in treatment. I believe that this is how all patients need to be addressed.

THE INFLUENCE OF INFANT RESEARCH ON SELF PSYCHOLOGY

As Kohutian theory gave psychoanalysis a more contemporary spin, it also began to resonate with and integrate some of the latest observational research coming out of child development. Self psychology was especially taken with infant research that looked at the role of mutual responsiveness and regulation between parent and child, and how active the infant was in seeking out what it needs.

Consequently, the Kohutian infant seems quite different from the Freudian infant. At the risk of oversimplifying, Freud's infant appeared to be more like a bundle of biological drives whose main foci were to have objects onto which it could discharge its drives, negotiate reality in order to reduce conflict, and maintain homeostasis.

Infant research suggested to self psychologists that a baby may already have a sense of boundaries between itself and others (Stern 1985). Yet it is a baby with initial connectedness to its selfobjects. Kohut's baby interacts more with its physical and psychological environment, perhaps starting in utero. When ties between the baby and its selfobject are disrupted, efforts are made by both to reestablish the self–selfobject tie. These efforts have been called "self-righting tendencies" (Tolpin 1986) that the infant later internalizes as a function of its own.

This baby's core self emerged from increasingly complex structures and functions in interaction with its selfobjects. These structures were partly determined by the kind of responsiveness gained from nurturing objects. The Kohutian baby was propelled to provide not only for its physical survival but also for the vitality and solidity of its self. It is a baby with an innate drive to become ever competent, to grow and actualize its talents and skills.

In developing self psychology, Kohut followed Freud's original belief that psychoanalysis should be a form of psychology and not a form of biology or sociology. As a consequence, he downgraded the role of the sexual and aggressive drives as prime motivators of personality development. Sexual(ized) and aggressive behaviors were now seen more as responses to failed efforts at getting others to respond to one's needs. A further consequence of Kohut's rethinking was that the concept of the oedipal complex was redefined. While Kohut was aware of the possible positive consequences of successfully negotiating the oedipal phase it was not central to core personality development as in structural theory. And rather than its being part of the normal development of the child, the oedipal complex was seen more as a child's symptomatic reaction to parents who were unattuned, during an important phase of the child's self development.

Many analytic thinkers divide the field into those analytic approaches that make the drive structure model pivotal, those that adhere to a relational model, and those that use a mixed model (Greenberg and Mitchell 1983). Ornstein (1991), one of the important self psychologists in the field and a major interpreter of Kohut, clearly believes that self psychology with its emphasis on how the self experiences the world is not a relational approach, even though the self is typically experienced in terms of its relationship to its selfobjects. Yet other self psychologists see this approach as needing to further evolve, and their contributions may incorporate more of an intersubjective or object relations approach. Ornstein points to part of the ongoing identity confusion stemming from Freud's seminal 1914 paper "On Narcissism," which he believed held the germs not only of ego psychology but of object relations and self psychology as well.

For therapists less theoretically oriented, these differences within the psychoanalytic schools may seem small and inconsequential in the face of the differences between the other major approaches, for example, the behavioral-cognitive, existential, Gestalt, and interpersonal schools, and between short-term and longer-term therapy.

THE SELF IN SELF PSYCHOLOGY

There are some aspects of self psychology that are particularly relevant to a short-term treatment approach. According to Kohutian theory (Kohut 1984, Ornstein 1978, Wolf 1988), the self is the core of the person's psyche around which increasingly complex structures and functions accrue. This metaphorical concept subsumes the Freudian concept of the ego. The infant's self emerges in the interaction among its genetic potential, environmental factors, and ongoing experience with early nurturing persons. Out of these interactions within this nascent self are believed to develop clusters of memories, affective patterns, cognitive-perceptual patterns of expectations, and various skills, such as affect regulation. By toddlerhood, these clusters become organized into the superstructure called the self. A healthy nuclear self is the center of initiative for the person and the repository of impressions. The care and growth of the person's own self is presumed to be the prime motivating force for the individual throughout life.

Early Kohutian theory elaborated the concept of the nascent or nuclear self as having a bipolar spatial structure within which were clustered ambitions and ideals. One's self was motivated by the push of its ambitions and the pull of its values and ideals. It was hypothesized that the nuclear self was pushed and pulled in both directions and influenced by the infant's innate talents and developed skills. How healthy the child's self became and the particular configuration of talents and skills that the child manifested depended on the psychological environment provided by its significant others over time.

For Kohut the self normally went beyond the boundaries of the physical body of the person to include the intrapsychic representations of its significant others. That is, the individual includes as part of its self those experiences provided by others that sustain the self. This refers to the self of a normal, healthy person as well as the self of a disturbed person. People include representations of others in their psyches throughout their lives.

A World of Selfobjects

Kohut believed that a person's self needed psychic nourishment for growth or maintenance, and that person would reach out to another person or thing—a selfobject—to obtain it. Psychically, selfobjects are experienced as part of one's self even though one is aware of being physically separate from them (except perhaps in acute psychotic or organic brain disorders). For this reason the word *selfobject* is cited as one word to reflect its place in the person's psyche. However, the definition of a selfobject is still evolving. Some therapists see the selfobject as a set of functions while others see it as a dimension of someone's experience.

Selfobjects are experienced by the self as providing psychological functions that sustain the self in terms of its cohesiveness and vitality, and help it to grow. In addition to people, ideas, symbols, and activities can provide selfobject functions. Selfobjects are so vital to a person's functioning that they are experienced as if they were part of the person, as, say, another arm that would do one's bidding. Thus when selfobjects don't respond to our needs tremendous anxiety and frustration can result.

Throughout life, from earliest infancy through old age, selfobject experiences are needed to nurture, help organize, and maintain the self. The dimensions of a healthy self include one that feels it is cohesive and bounded, and one that exists continuously over time so that it has a sense of sameness and resilient self-esteem.

In childhood the individual needs selfobject experiences to help organize and integrate the nascent self into a cohesive, functioning unit. These experiences provide the basis for enduring self-organization, self-esteem, and self-assertion, as well as affect regulation. These early selfobject experiences also set up patterns of what the child learns to expect regarding the responsiveness of the interpersonal environment.

The array of selfobject functions has been expanded from Kohut's original group to include more affective functions (see Stolorow et al. 1987) and cognitive-perceptual functions (Baker 1991). These involve facilitating in the individual the ability to differentiate, articulate, and integrate feeling states, perceptual-thought schemata, and expectations.

The individual continuously seeks out an environment of selfobject relationships into which to embed himself so as to ensure reliable response to his needs. However, the particular form that the selfobject needs and therefore the form that the selfobject experience takes change with the developmental age of the person.

Often, as we become adults we tend to look for more symbolic selfobject experiences than concrete ones. For example, when an adult in our culture is upset and needs soothing, the person usually chooses to be verbally stroked rather than physically stroked by someone or to engage in some activity, such as watching television, doing physical activity, or going shopping.

The Major Types of Selfobject Relationships

While human beings have many psychological needs, Kohut delineated several that specifically dealt with those experiences or relationships that were necessary for the maintenance or growth of the self. The frustration of early selfobject needs formed the basis of adult psychopathology. These needs would get reactivated in treatment in the form of specific transferences. The selfobject needs or selfobject relationships that are most commonly referred to and that manifest in selfobject transferences in therapy are mirroring, idealizing, and twinship.

Mirroring describes a relationship in which a selfobject provides the experience of unqualified acceptance of, esteem for, and interest in the other person. In childhood this includes an admiration and interest in the child's bodily self and accomplishments. An example of this experience is when a child is excited by his mastering of feeding himself with his spoon and the mother exclaims with matching feeling and body posture how wonderful it is that he can do this. For an adult, applause for a well-performed ballet is another form of mirroring.

A mirroring selfobject also "confirms the person's sense of vigor" (Goldstein 1990). When someone has the experience of being mirrored, it is internalized as a feeling of being more alive and solid inside. A person may feel more organized psychically and experience an increase in self-esteem. These experiences facilitate the person's pursuing his ambitions and interests.

The earliest version of a mirroring need is a merger need. For the person's self to feel vital and cohesive, it needs to feel completely one with a selfobject. While adults have moments of wanting a merger experience, when it is necessary in a sustained way for a person's self to thrive it is considered a sign of regression and disturbance.

Idealizing describes a prototypic relationship in which the individual is allowed the "experience of merging with a calm, strong, wise and good selfobject" (Wolf 1988, p. 126). For example, a person's self-esteem may be derived from being in the "reflective glow" of another person who is felt to be very powerful and competent. These experiences with one's caregivers facilitates a person's pursuing values and ideals as well as enabling the person to feel secure and soothed.

Twinship, a later concept of Kohut's, refers to a relationship in which the selfobject is perceived as a clone who is separate but identical to the self. The twin is experienced as a resonating alter ego, providing the self with a sense of connectedness and partnership. "One's perceptions are shared, not simply witnessed, by the twin" (Magdoff and Seruya 1994).

Since Kohut's initial work, Wolf (1988), Lichtenberg and colleagues (1992), and others have suggested additional important selfobject needs. Echoing some infant research, including White's (1959) theory of competence motivation, some self psychologists believe that there is need for the person to experience the self as having an impact on its selfobjects and to elicit the selfobject experiences the person gets from others. It has been referred to as a need for an "adversarial" selfobject experience. Here the individual experiences a selfobject as a benign and supportive but opposing force. The adversarial selfobject encourages an oppositional relationship in an effort to aid the autonomy and assertiveness of the individual.

Kohut believed that if these selfobject experiences, especially those related to mirroring, idealizing, and twinship, were provided consistently with nurturing figures, that would allow a person several chances for healthy, thriving development. When these experiences are not adequately provided, the self may resort to compensatory devices to bolster itself, or it may become vulnerable to states of depletion and fragmentation. We will see later how the selfobject dynamics originally established in childhood are later transformed and enacted in treatment with the therapist who provides, or acknowledges the need for, these functions.

When a human selfobject provides the infant with what it needs over time, at first physically and then psychologically, that selfobject is considered to be attuned to the infant's needs. Through interactions between the infant and its caregiver selfobjects, the infant begins to internalize the functions that its selfobjects provide. That process is called *transmuting internalization*. It was Kohut's belief that attuned responsiveness from one's earliest selfobjects was necessary for healthy personality development.

Early Kohutians believed that internalization of selfobject functions took place when the selfobject unintentionally failed to provide these functions and the infant was able to take these functions over. Ultimately, these functions become internalized in the other person as part of a healthy self structure that included healthy self-esteem, feelings of cohesiveness, feelings of joy, and "the ability to be self soothing, ambitious, creative and reasonably resilient" (Magdoff and Greenberg 1988).

In line with a belief that psychological experience is rarely a linear phenomenon, I suggest that these three selfobject needs probably oscillate within the person's psyche, with some in the background while others are in the foreground, or may even vie for dominance within the individual.

Reframing a Patient's Dysfunction

Wolf (1988) points out that a person's self functions in a fragile way to the extent that in early development the person did not receive the needed selfobject experiences from caregivers, or the experiences were inappropriate for that person (no matter how well intended the caregivers were). These experiences lead to an inadequate self structure. It is not a single trauma but a chronically faulty selfobject environment that impairs the self development of the child. For some people this leads to a more or less vulnerable self or, worse, to the incomplete development of self functions that would have enabled them to feel connected to the world and thrive in it. We tend to see more incomplete development of self structure and function in people with psychotic and borderline conditions.

Those with vulnerable selves may experience some kind of regression or impairment in functioning as a result of a breakdown in their current important self–selfobject relationships. When a person does manifest some dysfunction, self psychologists view subsequent symptoms, as well as various defenses and resistances, as the patient's best efforts to restore solidity and vitality to the self.

> Harry, divorced, and a successful vice president at a high technology firm, made a presentation of his next software idea. When he was told by his excited superiors, whom he respected, that his idea "is a go" he felt exhilarated, powerful, and solid inside.

The following month he presented another idea and his bosses looked puzzled over his concept and suggested he rework it and come back with it. At first he was confused, a little disoriented, and angry. At home these states gave way to feelings of humiliation and deflation and some gnawing sense of emptiness. His bosses were idealized selfobjects for him and they failed to affirm his worth in his eyes. In an effort to deal with his fragmented and deflated state, he started making a flurry of calls to a telephone sex line. While he resented feeling compelled to do something he viewed as unsavory, he knew these phone contacts would help him feel connected to some other human being and affirm he was worth someone's attention. At first very conflicted by these measures, he would feel soothed by a human voice interested in him, and then excited and alive once more.

This example points out another position that self psychology takes regarding pathology. In most classical analytic models, conflicts either between drives or between the agencies of the psyches are assumed to cause dysfunction. In self psychology, dysfunction is caused not so much by conflict but by a current failure of the selfobject environment to provide for a person who has some preexisting self vulnerability or deficit.

Kohut and Wolf attempted a classification system of selfobject relations disorders according to the nature and extent of the damage to the self (Wolf 1988). They defined the nature of self disorders within the psychoses, borderline states, narcissistic behavior disorders, narcissistic personality disorders, and within the psychoneuroses, which they considered a variant of the narcissistic personality disorders. In addition they described four commonly found pathological self states that crossed the various diagnostic groups, such as the understimulated or empty self, the fragmented self, the overstimulated self, and the overburdened self.

Wolf believes these self states result from a chronically misattuned selfobject environment that impeded the child's psychological development and left the child with a particular constellation of damage to the self. The understimulated or empty self state is due to an ongoing lack of joyful, stimulating response to the developing child. It results in a self state in which the person experiences boredom, a lack of vitality, and a lack of aliveness.

An overstimulated self state is usually the result of chronic, inaccurate, and excessive selfobject response on the part of the caregiver. With this kind of exposure, the person has a patterned difficulty in managing affects stirred up by fantasies of greatness or greatness of other selfobjects. In addition, the person may become shy and have difficulty in pursuing ambitious goals.

A person would tend to a self state of partial fragmentation as a result of caregivers' unintegrated, contradictory selfobject responses to the child's efforts to grow. One example is parents being overprotective of and competitive with their child at the same time. As an adult this person may tend to respond to selfobject misattunement by experiencing a lack of continuity in the sense of self. Wolf adds that these people seem particularly anxious and physically awkward.

The person who tends to overburdened self states had a childhood lacking in opportunities to connect to idealized calming figures. Wolf believes such people have great difficulty in soothing themselves and containing strong emotional states, so that they experience the world as dangerously overwhelming. Somatization is a common response to this experience.

Here is an example of a client manifesting dynamics of both the understimulated and overburdened self.

> Laura is a 50-year-old woman who came into treatment seeking help for the anxiety and depression she was experiencing as a result of a long-planned marital separation. She grew up in a small town with few friends and became quite reliant on her own inner life. Her father was a verbally abusive alcoholic and her mother chronically looked to her daughter for emotional grounding and support. Neither was available to shield her from the chronic tension in the home nor did they mirror their daughter's impressive musical talents. As a child she sometimes engaged in self-punishing physical acts and had fantasies of being rescued from her family by cinema heroes.
>
> We worked through her ambivalent reactions to the separation to her satisfaction, along with a significant reduction in her symptoms. She now found that while she was quite pleased with her new life, she had nothing to focus her thoughts on as she had with the separation. She was curious that she was now driven to engage in many work and creative activities, as she had done for so many years. She disclosed that such overactivity always made her feel more alive and better glued together inside.

Kohut and Wolf acknowledged that a true classification system needed to wait for more systematic data from clinicians of all kinds. Their contribution to understanding pathology may be in their outlining the inner experience of self disorders and identifying self states in particular.

The major pathways that disturbances in the self took related to the impact of stressors on the cohesiveness and on the vitality of the self. On the mild side, threats to the cohesiveness of the self could be experienced as a momentary ungluing of the self; for example, these people feel disoriented about time, have reduced attention and concentration and brief memory impairment, and don't quite feel like themselves. On the severe side, a person may feel completely fragmented in cognitive, perceptual, and affective processing and disconnected from her body. Here the sense of self is breaking up. Kohut believed this kind of fragmentation anxiety was one of the most dreaded experiences a person reported.

Threats to the self's integrity had a parallel impact on the vitality of the person's self. A mild threat could result in a person feeling temporarily deflated and mildly upset while a severe threat such as a difficult humiliation could make a person's self feel emptied out and deadened.

Reverberations of these threats to the self may lead to an array of symptomatic expressions, including affective reactions such as anger, envy, anxiety, shame, and depression. They may result in a host of intrapsychic defenses, or behaviors meant to shore up the person's sense of self. These efforts may be constructive efforts or self-defeating in the long run, but always reflect the urgent need of the person to restore the self.

Disruption in a self–selfobject relationship, a trauma, or a narcissistic injury are the major threats to the integrity of the self. The extent of their impact on the individual's self depends on the severity of the stress, the health of the person's self in terms of how cohesive and alive the person feels, and on the richness of the individual's selfobject support network. For example, a man may internally react to being fired from his job with glee, or with a minor upset, or with severe fragmentation of his self and depleting depression.

SELF PSYCHOLOGICAL ORIENTATION TO THERAPY

The general goals of therapy are to restore a client to a previous, adequate level of functioning, and/or to help the person get past blocks and to resume psychologically growing. They are accomplished through the cultivation of a self–selfobject relationship between the client and therapist that activates the reemergence of the client's thwarted selfobject needs. The clinician provides ongoing understanding and explaining (interpretation) of these needs. The therapist accepts and attempts to be responsive to these needs. The patient internalizes the selfobject functions that the therapist provides in their interpersonal interactions and resumes functioning.

The goal is not to replace selfobject relationships with object relationships but to replace archaic selfobject relationships with more flexible, developmentally appropriate ones. The focus involves enhancing the cohesiveness, continuity, and vitality of the self, that is, helping the patient build new psychological structure and/or develop compensatory mechanisms to aid functioning.

The therapist facilitates this first by providing a psychically safe environment in which the patient can explore inner experiences and where the therapist can become a useful selfobject. The self psychotherapist spends much time trying to understand the client by using empathic listening and inquiry. When the therapist believes she understands what the client is trying to express, she explains her understanding to the client.

The Role of Empathy in Treating Disorders of the Self

People can learn to become attuned and responsive to others by using their empathic skills. According to self psychology, empathy is a powerful and more accurate way of comprehending the resonating psychological state(s) of another person. Empathy is the result of putting oneself into the affective and cognitive experience zones of another person. It is often confused with sympathy, which entails trying to understand the experience of another through one's own experiences and values, and then acting in a compassionate manner. Empathy, however, entails trying to deeply understand the meaning of an event for a person based on that person's psyche, defense mechanisms, life experiences, and values.

When one empathically understands someone, a variety of responses may be offered, not just gentle kindness. Empathic comprehension of the client's needs and issues, however, is always corroborated by the therapist's gathering other forms of information about the client.

Ideally, once the therapist empathically comprehends some important issue for a client, the therapist tries to respond to the client in an attuned and optimal way for that situation. The therapist serves as a selfobject for the patient and provides needed selfobject functions. In so doing the therapist also role models for the patient how he can begin to provide those functions to his self or get others to provide them. The patient may also serve selfobject functions for the therapist.

Empathic Listening

The self psychologist identifies selfobject failures and self dysfunction through empathic listening. The clinician deliberately sustains an empathic stance throughout the treatment and makes efforts to immerse herself in the other person's thoughts and feelings always. The patient's experience of the therapist as empathic and attuned is particularly poignant for some people because it may be the first time the patient has been recognized by another in a way that makes her feel whole and alive.

From Optimal Frustration to Optimal Responsiveness

Kohut pushed back the boundaries of analytic neutrality and abstinence when he emphasized the need of the therapist to be emotionally responsive to the selfobject needs of the client. He theorized that psychological structure building took place at the interface in a therapeutic relationship where the therapist had been attuned enough to the patient to provide certain psychological functions but momentarily was unavailable or unattuned, that is, he optimally frustrated the patient. If the inevitable lack of attunement was experienced as manageable, then the patient took over these functions with the help of the therapist, who tried to repair the lapse in attunement. This structure-building process is the transmuting internalization process described above. It parallels initial development of the self of the growing infant.

Later self psychologists had a more controversial position regarding optimal frustration and what factors facilitated psychic structure. They referred to *optimal responsiveness* (Bacal 1985), and *facilitative responsiveness* (Lichtenberg et al. 1992), which also summarizes my clinical philosophy about helping people. While empathic understanding was deemed the key data-gathering instrument in self psychology, followers of Kohut formally acknowledged that empathic attunement to a patient's needs was in itself profoundly therapeutic, and further, that the therapist needs to be optimally responsive to the patient, which may involve not only interpreting what the patient needs but sometimes even judiciously providing it. Growth was seen as a result of the therapist's responsiveness and not only as a result of interpreting the patient's selfobject needs or as a result of frustration of those needs.

In this next vignette from the end phase of the short-term case of Laura we can see some of the major elements of self psychological theory and technique as it informed the therapy. Much of the time the therapist used empathic listening to understand the client and then to convey her acceptance and understanding of her. The therapist offered her understanding of Laura's underlying issues in terms of identification of selfobject needs. The therapist and client developed a self–selfobject relationship in which the therapist provided needed selfobject experiences to the patient. Some

repair of deficit was accomplished and a tendril of new psychological structure was appearing. In this session the therapist's acceptance of the patient's
self state was key.

Laura came in looking pale and tired from her job as a music teacher but
emotionally upbeat. She reported that she and her kids were now adjusting
well to living separately from a husband she had long ago stopped loving
and respecting. A few days earlier she had come back from her first vacation
weekend by herself in many years. She described once more doing a thou-
sand things to keep herself busy, which enabled her to feel more vital and
more intact.

During her vacation she realized that she loved interacting casually with
a lot of people. She never felt lonely, even at night, and enjoyed having no
one make demands of her. More than that she realized that she didn't want
to get emotionally intimate with anybody ever. We discussed it as a possible
reaction to her marital separation, but we both knew issues around intimacy
preceded her marriage. She knew that was an unpopular thing to say and
wondered what I thought of that. Sensing that this was an important moment, I told her that I didn't think she had to be like everybody else but I
would like to understand her attitude better. She explained her constant fear
was that she would be drained by the other's needs of her in an intimate relationship and she was just barely able to cope on her own. "On the outside
I look like all is well, I can perform, but on the inside I am withering away
from the demands." She then questioned the usefulness of looking at her
newly discovered fear of intimacy.

I replied that since she had felt she had practically dedicated her life to
satisfying others' needs while she went empty, I could understand why she
wouldn't want to disturb that wall. However, I thought that looking at this
dynamic would be helpful because if she felt she was just barely coping we
should address it. But I added that this may represent an old concept of her
self and set of expectations based on the draining and unsatisfactory relationships she experienced within her family. She began to wonder if it could
really be possible to expect others to give to her and not just take from her.
"How wild that would feel," she said. Her mood and body softened as she
shifted the topic.

She then smiled shyly and wistfully described having a rare dream. She
was on the western plains with Roy Rogers, who healed people with his
touch and was her hero. She recalled reveries where she would make herself light-headed by holding her breath and fantasizing about languishing
in some mountain pass. Roy would always find her and restore her breath-
ing. She'd march off with him and help him help the Indians. Perhaps the
therapist's validation of the client's need to protect herself and concern over

her difficulty in coping allowed her to reexamine this defense. As a result she could possibly move away from this distancing position and allow herself to consciously express a longing for an idealized figure who would want to be attuned to her needs.

Two sessions later she informed me that an eligible man had been expressing an interest in her for a while at work and that now she would consider meeting with him.

AN INTRODUCTION TO THE BRIEF PSYCHOTHERAPIES

In developing a framework for empathic brief treatment, my guiding theoretical and clinical attitude is self psychological. Aspects of other schools of therapy are incorporated to offer a new integration of theory and technique. Psychodynamic principles are melded with cognitive-behavioral concepts and techniques to maximize therapy effectiveness in a short time frame. This chapter focuses on individual psychotherapy. Chapter 7 discusses couples therapy.

For a comprehensive view of the myriad psychodynamic approaches to brief treatment the reader is referred to the work of Crits-Christoph and Barber (1991). Bloom (1992) surveys other possible approaches, including the interpersonal, cognitive-behavioral, existential, and strategic-systemic approaches.

DEFINING BRIEF THERAPY

Psychotherapy, across all the theoretical schools, may be seen as a process that can be broken down into stages. "These stages include the stage of: engagement, pattern search, change, and termination" (Beitman 1991, p. 24). Generic short-term psychotherapy follows that same basic path. It is defined as a form of therapy that is planned from the beginning to last generally from one to twenty-five sessions with an average of about ten sessions. The characteristics usually associated with short treatment are (1) circumscribed treatment goals, (2) the development and maintenance of a focus of treatment, (3) treatment that is rationed in some way (either by setting a time limit, session limit, or money limit, or all three), (4) rapid intervention of the therapist, and (5) high activity levels on the part of the therapist and client. Short-term therapists tend to recruit environmental resources to supplement in-session treatment. They are also more geared toward formally assessing the outcome of treatment than are longer-term therapists.

The schools of brief psychodynamic psychotherapy share the same features of brief treatment enumerated above. The many approaches to short-term dynamic therapy may include representatives from the schools of classical Freudian analysis, the neo-Freudian approaches, as well as the object relations, interpersonal, and self psychological schools.

In addition to the features previously identified, brief psychodynamic therapists share many other aspects in common. The theory of the development of psychopathology and treatment in brief therapy are informed by psychoanalytic principles developed by Freud and his followers. In general, psychodynamic therapists believe that the human personality is shaped by one's experiences in life as well as one's biological potential. Early life experiences are particularly formative of one's cognitive, affective, and behavior styles. All behavior is motivated and one's motives may not reach one's awareness. Psychological disturbance in any of these three spheres is the result of conflicting needs and drives.

Importance is given in psychodynamic treatment to (1) the therapeutic alliance and utilizing aspects of the transference and countertransference; (2) the use of psychoanalytic concepts, such as the role of psychic conflict, unconscious motivation, resistance, and defense mechanisms, as well as modified psychoanalytic techniques; (3) the patient selection criteria; and (4) the central role that termination plays in the therapy. Dynamic short-term therapists are likely to pay attention to repetitive maladaptive interpersonal patterns as well.

Key Concepts Used in Brief Dynamic Psychotherapy

The first three characteristics of generic short-term therapy clearly distinguish brief dynamic therapy from long-term, reconstructive, exploratory, analytic therapy. Realistic, doable goals are set and maintained throughout the brief, psychodynamic therapy process. The treatment goals are obtained by identifying and working on the focus of treatment. The goals of therapy and foci of treatment are usually agreed on formally by the client and therapist. Digressions from the focus of treatment are kept to a minimum so as to reach the important therapy goals. Unlike in longer-term psychoanalysis, free association is used for particular focal issues and is not the primary therapeutic tool.

Bauer and Kobos (1987) point out that the focus of treatment in brief therapy may be approached in many fashions, but each is an attempt to get to a core problem issue. For example, the focus of treatment may be a particularly troublesome "circumscribed symptom, an intrapsychic conflict or developmental impasse, a maladaptive conviction about the self . . . or a persistent interpersonal dilemma. . . . " (p. 157).

Many of the dynamic approaches to brief therapy are also based on the psychoanalytic principle of identifying a core conflict that may be the focus of treatment. This conflict is worked through by the therapist's aggressively analyzing unconscious material, usually of an oedipal nature, and by analyzing the resistance and the transference. The therapist focuses on a particular conflict and places other material in the background.

Another hallmark of analytic brief therapists, such as Davanloo (1978), Sifneos (1979), and Malan (1976), is the use of transference interpretations termed the *triangle of conflict* and the *triangle of insight*. It is around these kinds of interventions that much of brief psychodynamic therapy revolves.

The idea of the triangle of insight was likely developed by Alexander (1956), refined by Menninger (1958), and then further modified by Davanloo (1978). Shortly we will look at the contributions of these therapists in more detail. Traditionally, transference interpretations relate the patient's experiences happening in the current interaction between therapist and patient to their origins in the patient's history of significant relationships (usually with parental figures). In using the metaphor of the triangle of insight the therapist makes transference interpretations linking up patterns of how the patient is reacting with the therapist to how the patient behaves in other current life situations as well as to the patient's behavior in past significant relationships. Insight obtained by looking at this triangle should be emotionally meaningful to the patient since it encompasses behavior, attitudes, and feelings. By connecting the different sources of the patient's inner experience, these therapists enlarged the scope of the transference interpretation and made it a more powerful therapeutic tool.

Many brief therapists believe that such interpretations should be offered very early and aggressively in the treatment. When done early, responses to such trial interpretations may be used to decide if the patient is appropriate for this kind of therapy. These interpretations also serve slightly different functions in empathic brief therapy. Here the trial interpretations are framed in the language and concepts of self psychology. Responses to the triangular interpretations are used by the therapist to refine the level on which the patient needs to be addressed rather than to determine if the patient is inappropriate for treatment.

From the view of empathic brief therapy the triangle of insight is a useful tool. It gives the therapist a way to focus on the clinical material and to organize her interventions. Employing the triangular interpretation also addresses the inner and outer experiences of the patient in a more multidimensional and integrated way. However, in making the triangular linkages, the empathic therapist needs to be mindful that the transference reaction is the result of the interplay between two subjective psyches—that of the patient and that of the therapist. Likewise, when the patient is experiencing someone in his current life as he would some significant person from his past it is probably because there is something about that current person that is evocative of the past, internalized relationship.

Additionally, the ultimate goal of empathic brief therapy is not just insight but should include (1) the start of internalizing the therapist's functions, such as improved affect regulation, increased energy, and entitlement to pursue goals; or (2) helping the patient to create a more sustaining self–selfobject environment.

The triangle of conflict refers to a way of conceptualizing what happens for the patient in his troubled interactions with other people. The triangle represents the dynamic relationship between the patient's impulses and the anxiety/guilt associated with the repressed feelings threatening to break through to consciousness, and to the defensive patterns used to ward off the untoward impulses. Dynamic therapists may apply the triangle of conflict to each of the client's troubled interpersonal relationships identified in the triangle of insight. Therapist and client together explore and work on the client's maladaptive patterns.

Again, using the two triangles conjointly is a valuable heuristic tool. They provide a quick and graphic way for the therapist to understand some of the patient's issues. The triangles also provide a structure by which the client can work on issues outside of the sessions. Yet these concepts represent a simplified model of all that goes on internally for a person at any point in time.

The triangles as used by many dynamic therapists are also more interpersonally oriented. Other people in the patient's world are assumed to be psychically separate from the patient, so that often oedipal-level dynamics are the focus. Self psychological brief treatment always addresses the internal, intrapsychic state of the client first, which is presumed to be more at the core of the person's psychological foundation, and then proceeds to the interpersonal.

Self psychotherapists view the person's intrapsychic dynamics differently, which would modify the elements in the triangle of conflict. An important object, that is, a selfobject, may not even be a person. The self psychological model is need- and deficit-based rather than conflict-based, so it does not fit into a triangle as easily. The chain of intrapsychic-interpersonal reactions is more multidimensional, with nodal inner experiences causing several responses and defensive counterreactions in turn. Graphically not as neat, this is a sequence in which the disturbance starts with the client's experiencing some break in the support afforded by a self–selfobject relationship or with a trauma. The client may experience herself as not as cohesive or solid inside, or as becoming drained of energy. She may react to those symptoms with increased anxiety, rage, shame, and dread of further debilitating depression. She will then make efforts to stem the spreading impact of the disturbance and restore cohesion and vitality to herself. Her attempts may be healthy or include symptomatic efforts. In a self psychologically informed therapy, the therapist allows the patient to have another self–selfobject experience with the therapist that will aid the patient in restoring her self.

In a disturbed interaction with another person, rather than focusing on repressed thoughts and feelings as the internal psychic engine, self psychotherapists focus on affective and cognitively formed need states having to do with self cohesion and self vitality. Instead of looking at anxiety and guilt as responses to fears of repressed material emerging, we speak of the fear of states of deflation, shame, emptiness, and fragmentation resulting if a person's needs are not addressed appropriately. The defenses used to ward off feared or impending states of deflation or fragmentation may include anger and other internal states, or may be behavioral patterned ways of coping.

Differences among the Psychodynamic Approaches

Within the psychodynamic school of time-limited psychotherapy there is some important variability among its practitioners both in their attitudes toward brief therapy and in how they practice it. Some practitioners think it should always be the treatment of choice since it is perceived to be as effective as longer-term therapy. Others feel it is more limited than longer-term therapy but useful. Still others are dubious about the value of brief therapy but are required to work within a rationed framework. In addition, therapists differ in how widely applicable their approach is. Some therapists believe their approach is useful for the general population while others feel their approach is specific to some kinds of problems or diagnostic categories.

Bloom (1992) points out several areas in which brief therapists vary in terms of their practice: length of treatment and number of sessions (where external factors do not impose a time limit), use of a therapeutic contract with the client regarding the goals of therapy, and how active they are in session and how disclosing.

Therapists also vary in the degree to which they use confrontation, offer support, or encourage exploration. Many dynamic therapists encourage and use the positive transference developed in treatment. The use of the negative transference varies greatly and evokes strong responses among therapists and patients. Many therapists doing brief therapy try to prevent or minimize the development of a negative transference. Brief therapists vary also in the importance they give to interpersonal factors versus intrapsychic factors in developing pathology as well as in the goals of the therapy.

Therapists also vary in the use of follow-up interviews of treatment, which often consist of one in-person, phone, or written interview. Evaluation of treatment outcome also varies, with some therapists not doing it at all, others having patients informally evaluate their own progress, and still others informally rating the progress or using formal assessment studies. There is a trend for posttreatment steps to be taken more seriously.

History of Brief Dynamic Therapy

The history of brief dynamic therapy is often broken down into four chronological generations (Crits-Christoph and Barber 1991, Levenson and Butler 1994). Earlier generations tended to conceptualize therapy using a drive/structural model. Later generations tend to use a relational model or models incorporating a mixture of approaches. Marmor (1979) and Bauer and Kobos (1987) provide a thorough historical review.

First Generation

In the first generation are most commonly placed the contributions of Freud, Ferenczi, Rank, and Alexander and French. Freud's work provided the foundation for both short-term and long-term psychodynamic psychotherapy. In the late 1880s Freud moved away from using hypnosis in his efforts to treat people with mental disorders. In collaboration with Breuer he developed a form of psychotherapy that was expected to be brief in duration and that acknowledged the curative role of the therapist–patient relationship. By 1895 he and Breuer attempted to articulate the dynamics and treatment of their patients in their *Studies on Hysteria*. Bauer and Kobos (1987) point out that in this book Freud and Breuer focused on several aspects of treatment deemed essential to short-term therapy today. These included the importance placed on patient selection criteria, a solid therapeutic alliance, sustained and aggressive attention to patient resistance, and maintaining a treatment focus.

Some noteworthy examples of Freud's brief psychotherapy included the successful treatment of the conductor Bruno Walter in six sessions and of the composer and conductor Gustav Mahler in one four-hour session. Training analyses at this time also were often conducted in under one year. In his early work Freud believed that insight into the origin of a neurotic problem would quickly resolve it. This frequently meant focusing on one symptom at a time and eliminating it.

By 1905 Freud's concept of the psyche had changed and become more complex. Free association was an important therapeutic agent. In conducting an analysis he became as interested in advancing the science of the mind as he was in the treatment of the disorders of the mind. As a result, over the years Freudian treatment got longer, more complex, and more ambitious. For example, as Freud developed the concept of resistance it became necessary to lengthen treatment to resolve resistance to change. Malan (1963) notes that less emphasis was placed on symptom resolution and more on interpretations and the complete working through of transference material. Freud felt that treatment with those of his patients he described as severely ill now took between half a year and three years, while for less disturbed people it should take less time. However, he still saw the value in shorter treatment if its outcome was positive for the patient.

By 1913 Freud was becoming increasingly skeptical of the effectiveness of brief therapy. He felt that the enduring and deep changes in the mind required a longer period of time for the analytic process. The longer length of time for therapy cases was also needed to glean more information for the science of psychoanalysis.

During these years some in Freud's analytic circle began to express concern over the growing length of treatment. Several, such as Ferenczi, Rank, and Alexander, tried to put forth their own contributions to psychoanalysis on such topics as the length of therapy and activity level of the analyst, but they were rejected from the circle. Freud believed emphatically that psychoanalysis should continue to evolve and that more efficient methods be found to help people, but he had little tolerance for others' feedback on how to accomplish these goals.

By 1937, when Freud published *Analysis Terminable and Interminable*, he had jettisoned the idea of brief psychotherapy. He was also less optimistic about psychoanalysis successfully curing people. He believed that some part of the client's intrapsychic conflicts would always remain inaccessible to treatment and that resolved conflicts might reemerge in later years. He recommended, therefore, that analysts go back into personal therapy every four to five years. (Interestingly, brief therapists today often talk about the usefulness of intermittent therapy throughout life [Siddall et al. 1988]. They acknowledge that their goals each time are narrowly focused and that different developmental stages bring their own challenges.) Freud's death in 1939 and the war neuroses developed during World War II may have led to the reemergence of interest in brief treatment.

Ferenczi (1921) was one of the first psychoanalysts to experiment with creating a shortened and more effective psychoanalysis. His prescient focus was on increasing the activity level in the therapy process and on exploring the therapeutic qualities of the analyst–patient relationship. Ferenczi felt he could obtain better results in therapy if the therapist and patient were both more active in the treatment. He also pointed out that much of what was defined as the passive therapist posture was really an active one, such as when silence was employed.

His techniques anticipated approaches advocated by later schools of psychotherapy (both analytic and behavioral). For example, Ferenczi encouraged patients to experience activities and thoughts they avoided, and he prohibited them from engaging in compulsive behaviors, in order to heighten their awareness and anxieties, which could then be available for analysis. During free association he would have his clients fantasize about material that emerged. Ferenczi viewed therapy more as a two-person process and strongly encouraged analysts to explore how their interventions affected the patient's behavior. In his study of the analyst–patient relationship Ferenczi identified the process that would later be known as the technique of countertransference analysis and interpretation. He also set a time limit to treatment.

He believed that the therapy approach should be basically analytic but be tailored to the individual needs of each patient especially if the therapy was stagnating. Ferenczi indicated that using these active techniques required good therapeutic skills. Since they would affect the developing transference, they should be used only after a solid therapeutic alliance developed.

In his later work Ferenczi tried to improve the outcome of psychoanalysis by making therapy more of an emotional experience than an intellectual one. Paralleling his technique of heightening anxiety for analytic purposes, he developed a relaxation technique that enabled the patient to feel safe enough to express a fuller range of thoughts and feelings. Interpretations were to be framed in a tactful, empathic manner rather than in an authoritarian one. He even experimented with physical contact with patients to provide them with a reparative experience for the traumas that he believed affected their psychological development. These experiments brought the condemnation of the analytic community on his entire approach. However, Ferenczi's contributions to a more effective and humanistic psychotherapy have been incorporated by therapists today.

Rachman (1989) acknowledges Ferenczi's pioneering work: "There are several basic concepts that bear comparison between Ferenczi and Kohut: (1) the role of empathy in psychoanalysis; (2) the selfobject transference; (3) reintroduction of the trauma theory; and (4) revision of the resistance model" (p. 89).

Rank worked alone and in collaboration with Ferenczi to streamline and improve the effectiveness of psychoanalysis. They both felt that the therapy should focus on more of the current events in the life of the patient and be a more active experience for both therapist and patient. His own work foreshadowed concepts and techniques later employed by short-term therapists. For example, Rank was one of the early analysts to look at level of motivation for change as an indicator of therapy success. This was derived from his work on the concept of will. He also emphasized that patients should be helped to express their feelings and thoughts rather than therapists foreclosing on these experiences with their own interpretations. He viewed resistance in therapy as a possible effort on the part of the patient to express some tendril of independence.

His theory of birth trauma was widely rejected, but important aspects of it remain. From this exploration it became clear that separation was an important issue for people, especially in treatment. Setting termination dates became a way to place this issue in the forefront of treatment. In addition, his exploring the role of the birth trauma helped turn analysts' interest to the preoedipal period of development and the importance of the role of mothering and nurturance.

Despite the early unpopularity of short-term therapy among psycho-analysts, World War II pressed therapists to treat the returning traumatized soldiers quickly. At this time Alexander and French (1946) published *Psychoanalytic Therapy: Principles and Applications*, which many view as the first manual of short-term therapy. They built on the work of Ferenczi and Rank and questioned many of the basic tenets of psychoanalysis. They challenged the idea that increased frequency and length of treatment were required for a successful therapy. Instead they believed that people could be adequately helped in much shorter periods, especially if treatment was well planned. They discouraged the therapist from behaving as a blank screen, and they made the experience more interpersonal. Alexander also made an important distinction between regression in therapy that was helpful to the therapy process and regression that made working on current tasks more difficult. It was important for patient selection and the course of treatment that the two types of regression be distinguished.

The therapist should be flexible in helping the patient and tailor the treatment to the needs of the patient in the different phases of treatment, especially in terms of level of emotional intensity induced in each session. Flexibility also meant one could adjust the number of sessions per week, incorporate planned interruptions of treatment, vary the use of couch or chair, and even combine psychotherapy with other treatment modalities. These efforts were aimed at reducing patient dependency, controlling the transference neurosis, and maximizing therapy effectiveness.

Alexander and French believed in the primacy of emotional experience over intellectual activities in therapy, which became the keystone of their approach. The therapist facilitated a reparative "corrective emotional experience" with the patient as a way of overcoming past traumata. In therapy the therapist reexposed the patient to part of the emotional trauma that was interfering with her functioning. Within the safety of this relationship the therapist would respond to the patient in a more appropriate way than did the persons who induced the trauma. The patient might still respond in an outdated fashion. These perceptions and responses would be explored and worked through, and the patient's ego would then integrate this new kind of responsiveness and information.

Second Generation

The second generation of short-term dynamic psychotherapy occurred between 1960 and 1980. Beginning with the works of Malan, Sifneos, Mann, and Davanloo, brief dynamic therapy was considered a legitimate treatment option.

Malan developed his approach, which is considered a form of applied psychoanalysis, while working with Michael Balint and his cohorts (Ornstein and others) in England. (In a later chapter we will discuss this group's approach as one of the possible forerunners of a brief self psychological approach.) Their joint development of a short-term, psychoanalytically oriented therapy was termed *focal therapy* and later *intensive brief psychotherapy*. Malan took the radical position that he could bring about depth change even in those with severe psychopathology if they were appropriately selected and had therapy geared to their needs. The keys to this approach are a careful, extensive selection process, an active therapist who identifies a focal goal of treatment with the patient, a thoroughly planned treatment, and assessment of therapy outcome.

The selection process consisted of conducting an initial psychodynamic evaluation and screening out patients inappropriate for his form of therapy. During the evaluation process he went beyond history taking to include trial interpretations as a way to assess patient appropriateness in terms of level of insight and motivation for this kind of treatment. As a result, trial interpretations have become a part of many dynamic approaches as well as the triangles of conflict and insight that he introduced. Also during this evaluation time the therapist identified a focal problem, that is, some circumscribed aspect of a nuclear (childhood derived) conflict that could be worked through in a short period of time.

With the patient's agreement about the focal issue, the therapist concentrated in the first phase on identifying the triangle of conflict around it. In the middle phase, work centered on transference interpretations using the triangle of insight. Malan employed sensitive interpretations that went deep but were limited to the circumscribed focal problem. The final phase centered on feelings around termination and bringing in nuclear conflict and transference interpretations as they related to termination. Malan set therapy limits in terms of a date rather than number of sessions and would offer intermittent sessions after termination (tune-ups).

Echoing Rank's work on the importance of separation issues, Mann (1973) developed a short-term treatment (*time-limited treatment*) approach in which issues around separation, the impermanence of relationships, and losses were the cornerstone. Adherence to a twelve-session limit was absolute to maximize analytic access to these issues. Therapy consisted of a more adaptive reliving with the therapist of the reunion and separation from failed early caregivers. The particular separation conflicts that would be the focus of treatment were usually determined after a few sessions. The patient would then work through issues of guilt and ambivalence, anger and abandonment with those failed caregivers. Only those able to tolerate the upheaval associated with termination and the ability to manage strong affective reactions were recommended for this approach.

Sifneos (1979) developed *short-term anxiety-provoking therapy* as Malan was working on his approach at Tavistock in the 1960s. Sifneos developed techniques that were based on analytic principles to help people with relatively stable ego functions to work through oedipal-level issues in a short period of time. To start, his selection criteria were even more stringent and explicit than those of other approaches. Clients needed to have a circumscribed problem, a demonstrated ability to have a meaningful relationship, high intelligence, psychological flexibility during the intake, access to affects, above average psychological sophistication, and motivation to change.

Along with the patient, a focus of treatment was established regarding the specific unresolved oedipal conflicts to be addressed. As a focus of treatment was established, Sifneos specified in detail what a successful outcome of treatment would be. During the evaluation Sifneos would work quickly to establish a solid therapeutic alliance and elicit transference feelings. With that in place, he would aggressively confront the patient with transference feelings and make interpretations early in treatment regarding the therapist–parent connection.

Manifestations of transference neurosis, patient dependency, and acting out were to be quickly addressed and then avoided. This therapy was not supportive but rather used confrontation and anxiety-inducing questions to heighten emotional intensity to work on the focal oedipal issue. In this state the patient would be better able to understand the nature of his conflicts, identify the maladaptive defenses he used to cope, and ultimately to have "a corrective emotional experience." Sifneos emphasized that therapy wasn't just about the patient learning about himself but also about developing problem-solving skills. Treatment averaged four months. Afterward, outcome specifications were assessed by an independent evaluator.

While Sifneos was viewed as a therapist/tough schoolmaster, Davanloo (1978) viewed himself as the "relentless healer." His approach, *intensive short-term dynamic psychotherapy*, was influenced by the works of Malan and Sifneos, with whom he collaborated on research. His work is also based on analytic principles but requires a very active therapist. The evaluation process is the first phase of treatment. Like the other brief therapists mentioned, Davanloo screened and interviewed prospective patients thoroughly. In the interview he conducted aspects of a therapy session, including interpretations (trial therapy), to assess the appropriateness of the patient for treatment. His other criteria, similar to those of Sifneos, emphasized the ability of the patient to tolerate intense affects and thoughts. Patients accepted for treatment might have chronic problems of an oedipal nature, of loss, or of chronic neurotic characterological difficulties or symptoms. His therapy averaged between ten and fifteen sessions.

Davanloo treated patients by continuously confronting and then interpreting their resistances and defenses. Interpretations were formed around the triangles of conflict and insight and often looked at the role of patient anger. Negative transference was addressed and defused promptly as well as any symbiotic transference manifestations. Cure was derived through the uncovering and reexperiencing of the identified oedipal level conflict. Therapy outcome was assessed by a therapist interview, an independent evaluator, and by the patient immediately after termination and then five years later.

Third Generation

The third generation of brief therapies are also psychoanalytically informed. However, they are much more interpersonally oriented and more likely to conceptualize the genetic link between nuclear conflicts and current dysfunction from an object relations, Sullivanian, or ego psychological perspective rather than a classical one. The focus of treatment is on maladaptive issues in the patient's interpersonal relationships. To that end much work is done with the transference relationship since it is assumed to mirror other troubled relationships in the patient's current life.

In addition, this generation of brief therapists has conducted more rigorous research to both validate the effectiveness of and identify the major therapeutic factors in a successful brief therapy. As a result of the effort to assess the new approaches, brief treatments became more standardized and manualized, which had its own advantages and drawbacks.

The major representatives of this group include Horowitz's (1976) *short-term dynamic therapy for stress response syndromes*, Luborsky's (1984) *supportive-expressive psychotherapy*, Strupp and Binder's (1984) *time-limited dynamic psycho-*

therapy, Weiss and Sampson's (1986) *control mastery theory*, and Benjamin's (1991) application of her structural analysis of social behavior to brief therapy, called *reconstructive learning therapy*. Crits-Christoph and Barber (1991) provide good details of these major contributors.

Beth Israel Hospital in New York should also be noted for the research on brief psychotherapy done there as well as approaches to brief therapy developed from clinicians who have worked there, such as Jerome Pollack, Michael Laikin, Arnold Winston, Manuel Trujillo, Leigh McCullough, Henry Pinsker, and Walter Flegenheimer.

Fourth Generation

Levenson and Butler (1994) refer to a fourth generation of brief therapy, coexisting with the prior two generations, representing all the current approaches that attempt to address the socioeconomic and sociocultural factors affecting health care today. There is even greater stress on standardized brief approaches that a clinician can be reliably trained in, one that can be researched and assessed. More of these therapies incorporate theoretical orientations of several schools and are practically oriented.

Levenson and Butler suggest that many of the current models of brief treatment require longer-term treatment than managed care will allow. I believe, along with therapists like Jill Gardner, Miriam Elson, and Howard Baker, that self psychology can be adapted to short-term work and even to managed care work. There is a general trend for the theoretical emphasis in brief treatment to go from the intrapsychic to the interpersonal. Brief self psychotherapy would seem to fall somewhere in the middle.

COGNITIVE-BEHAVIORAL THERAPY

Cognitive-behavioral therapy, as the name implies, represents the union of two distinct approaches to therapy that took place over the last two decades. Both focus on modifying a person's behavior. To put it oversimply, cognitive-behavior therapy deals with the impact of our cognition, that is, thoughts, beliefs, expectations, on our emotions and subsequent behaviors. There are short-term, planned approaches to cognitive-behavioral therapy as well as longer-term versions of this school. However, even the longer-term approaches tend to be much shorter than most psychodynamic approaches.

Cognitive-behavioral therapy is included in this chapter on brief therapy for several reasons. This discussion provides some background on the cognitive-behavioral techniques that empathic brief psychotherapy employs. Also, cognitive-behavioral therapy has proven to be quite effective for a range of disorders, especially those related to anxiety and depressions (Phillips 1985). Further, cognitive-behavioral therapy, now in its third generation, may be developing some clinical and theoretical convergence with psychodynamic approaches.

Originally, Pavlovian, stimulus-response conditioning and Skinnerian operant conditioning led the way for a theory of psychopathology and psychotherapy based on addressing overt behavior called behavior therapy. The early, radical behaviorist position was that all behavior, including pathology, was controlled by external environmental contingencies. The mind was left unexplored. Decades later, while Kohut was developing his work on the narcissistic disorders, behavior therapy began to incorporate social learning theory and look at internal processes of the mind that mediated behavior.

Psychology's interest in cognitive activity, with its early studies of the role of values, purpose, will, and anticipation of the future, goes back to its days as a nascent science. But it wasn't until the 1970s that cognitive theory, with its focus on information processing, expectations, and appraisal concepts, became the rage in scientific psychology; some say it began a revolution.

At this time dissatisfaction was growing with the inadequacies of behavior therapy in addressing both psychopathology and behavior change. The works of such important cognitive therapists as Albert Ellis, Aaron Beck, and the multimodal approaches of Richard and Arnold Lazarus emphasized the role of affective and cognitive processes in understanding pathology and bringing about behavior change. Staunch behaviorists at first rejected the incursion of interest in cognitive factors in human behavior. But later cognitive theory and therapy were integrated with the behavioral clinical approach to form a hybrid cognitive-behavioral approach. However, there are still adherents to each school alone.

Meichenbaum (1993), a cognitive-behaviorist, suggests that cognitive-behavioral therapists have struggled with "how best to conceptualize their clients' cognitions and how to fit such cognitive processes into the complex reciprocal interrelationships with clients' feelings, behavior, and resultant consequences, as well as with the physiological and socio-cultural processes" (p. 202). While he refers to cognitive-behavioral therapists specifically, I believe that *all* therapists must struggle with how to integrate these same micro- and macroprocesses when attempting to understand and help patients.

Meichenbaum goes on to discuss chronologically the three guiding metaphors used in cognitive-behavior therapy's history. At first, cognitive-behaviorists viewed thoughts as covert behaviors (coverants) that were subject to traditional laws of conditioning and learning. Therapy involved deconditioning maladaptive thoughts and developing new adaptive thought patterns and skills.

Cognitive-behavior therapists then turned to the analogy of mind as computer. Cognitive dynamics were framed in terms of information processing theory and social learning theory. Cognition consisted of such processes as encoding, decoding, attributional biases, attentional factors, and cognitive errors (distortion mechanisms).

Cognitive structures or schemata such as enduring thoughts, beliefs, attitudes, and expectancies mediated affect and influenced how behavior was affected by external events. In turn, these internal cognitive processes and capacities were built up by prior experiences. Cognition even mediated the person's responses and adjustment to his environment. Dysfunction would result from particular kinds of patient expectations and repetitive self statements that tended to become self fulfilling. For example, patients were thought to experience depression because their distorted thinking led to a distortion of reality and because they held onto illogical beliefs. But such cognitive activity could be monitored and altered by therapy.

Interventions included interruptions of the cycle of cognitive-affective-behavioral patterns and the substitution of more adaptive coping responses. A large number of cognitive-behavior therapists use this second metaphor and therapy approach quite successfully. Cognitive-behavior therapies here tend to focus on three major areas: (1) coping skills, which represent a collection of techniques that focus on helping the patient develop a repertoire of skills with which to cope in stressful situations; (2) cognitive restructuring methods, which assume that maladaptive thoughts cause emotional stress, so that treatment intervenes to establish more adaptive thought patterns; and (3) problem-solving skills, a combination of the two above and which "emphasize the development of general strategies for dealing with a broad range of personal problems and stress the active collaboration between therapist and patient in planning the treatment program" (Dobson 1988, p. 13).

The latest metaphor that Meichenbaum (1993) refers to is used by many other kinds of short-term therapists who use a mixed theoretical model for conducting therapy (Hoyt 1994). The new metaphor is partially the result of several new trends in science and philosophy, including the influences of the concepts of constructivism, systems theory, self-organization theory, social learning theory, attachment theory, human development theory, and theories on the basic processes of change.

This new, postmodern metaphor has a different philosophical base, that is, social-constructivism, rather than the logical-positivistic orientation of earlier science. As a group the therapies based on this metaphor are referred to as the solution-focused, competency-based, constructive therapies. However, members of the schools of psychoanalysis are also incorporating aspects of this newer orientation in their field of inquiry and therapy.

Cognitive-behavioral therapists believe that through symbolic activity of the mind human beings create their own personal view of the world so that each person has his own reality. Now the therapist's job is to help patients be aware of the reality they are creating, the consequences of their constructions, and as co-constructivist, to help alter their patients' maladaptive stories. The role of affect and interpersonal relationships attain more importance in this kind of therapy, too.

For Meichenbaum, the first phase of constructivist treatment requires that the therapist listen empathically and nonjudgmentally. A number of clinical techniques are used to help the patients tell what happened to them and why. Stressful events are reframed so that the role of symptoms is demoted from being the cause of their dysfunction. Instead, the stories they construct of their experience are identified as the major cause of the problems. Symptoms are viewed as understandable, spontaneous efforts at adapting.

The therapist helps the patient identify the elements of chronic stressors to enable her to use problem-solving tools and affective management devices. The therapist helps the patient to use what psychological resources she has, and helps develop new ones. In this process patients start to develop new assumptions of the world and new images of themselves.

Some of the constructivist tenets bear similarities to those of self psychology, including the reference to the sustained interplay of the subjective realities of the therapist and patient during a session that creates a unique therapy experience for both, the use of empathy and a nonjudgmental attitude, the importance of the therapeutic relationship, the view of symptoms as attempts at repair, and an optimistic, growth-oriented attitude in therapy rather than a pathological one.

In these ways empathic brief psychotherapy is also consistent with a constructivist short-term therapy approach. In both there is a blending of focus on the intrapsychic and interpersonal as well as allowing the therapist to be seen as an imperfect human being, with needs and reactions. Countertransference is viewed as inevitable and a contribution to the treatment, where both the therapist's and patient's realities interact with each other rather than be dichotomized.

As a school of short-term therapies, cognitive-behavior treatment is reeducative in that the therapeutic model is usually explained to the patient and the therapeutic rationale for each intervention is detailed. It is time limited and often limited in the target of change. In its emphasis on solutions, it tends to be present and future oriented. To that end there is little interest in exploring the genetic determinants of symptoms. With a positive attitude about change, the therapist encourages the patient to use the resources he has and to keep in mind situations when he had been effective with a problem and not just when there were failures.

One of the major flaws I find in the earlier, more established cognitive-behavior theories is that cognition comes first and is always thought to organize and mediate affect and behavior. More current research shows that all three have reciprocal, mediating relationships. Dobson (1988) provides a fairly complete summary of the established major cognitive-behavioral approaches.

Bloom (1992) summarizes the work of some of the major players in the field of short-term cognitive-behavior therapy. They are Ellis's *rational-emotive psychotherapy*, Phillips and Wiener's *structured behavior change therapy*, Beck's *cognitive restructuring therapy*, Erikson's *brief strategic psychotherapy*, and Farrelly's *provocative therapy*. However, Hoyt (1994) presents several innovative therapists who incorporate cognitive-behavioral elements in their form of constructive therapy as well.

INTEGRATING COGNITIVE-BEHAVIORAL ELEMENTS WITH SELF PSYCHOLOGY

I endorse some of the therapeutic attitudes of the cognitive-behaviorists as well as some of the techniques, including the belief that therapy should be growth oriented and positively oriented, and that clients should be encouraged to actively use their resources in their own behalf. I agree that small therapeutic changes or gains are psychological beachheads and should not be downplayed. These efforts can have impact on the client's psychological functioning in far-reaching ways that may not be immediately evident. People can behave themselves into new ways of thinking and feeling and vice versa. Insight is not the only path to therapeutic success.

Using empathic listening I attempt to enter the world of the client and try to understand how that person constructs her world in terms of her core expectations of herself and others. We look at her fixed beliefs, especially negative ones, and how they may become exaggerated and generalized. We also offer to the client examples of her having positive experiences.

The kinds of cognitive and behavioral techniques I may employ in treatment include relaxation training, guided visual imagery, role playing, behavioral rehearsal, stopping of chronic maladaptive thoughts, and challenging distorted thoughts and expectations of self and others. I try to help modify a patient's negative self concept by getting him to recall positive examples of situations where he was able to be effective. When necessary I also teach the patient how to problem solve.

These concrete techniques are usually meant to assist the empathic work around disabling anxiety, depression, obsessions, and compulsions. An overview of my approach might look like the following: my first task is to use empathy to understand the underlying cause of a client's pain or dysfunction and how it affects the state of her self experience. I work on becoming a reparative selfobject and teach patients to recruit other selfobjects into their world. Symptoms are reframed as efforts to adapt. In conveying my self psychological understanding I include interpretations of the negative impact that selfobject failures have not just on their affective state but also on their thinking and expectations of their self and others. Then I link up the behavioral consequences of the selfobject failures. Beyond understanding, I facilitate clients' learning to alleviate their symptoms. This symptom work takes priority in treatment especially if symptoms interfere with the work on the focal problem.

Here is an example of my integration of self psychotherapy and cognitive-behavioral treatment.

Henry was a 60-year-old single man who worked as a legal paraprofessional. He came into therapy because he was painfully inhibited in meeting people, especially women, and was taking courses to change his career. The previous session he described feeling somewhat abandoned during the holidays since no one he knew was around. However, what was different this year was that for both Memorial Day and July 4th, a man he knew from a self-help group invited him to his parties. Rather than do his normal rejection of offers to socialize and withdraw, he accepted. This change that he was so pleased about stemmed partly from our work of previous sessions where I encouraged him to try out new social situations just for the experience of change. At the July 4th party he met a beautiful but shy woman who had a deformed finger, which she hid. For the first time in his life he was helping someone else feel less self-conscious at a party. He felt so good at the party that he feared he might be coming on too strong. I mirrored his pride at overcoming his self-consciousness and added how good it must feel to be able to behave so confidently, which was new for him. In my accentuating the positive he could then get in touch with even more excited and optimistic feelings about himself. I decided to look at his anxious reaction a little later as a kind of defensive undoing.

In the next session he started out describing how much better he felt this week. Both in his personal and professional life he felt more competent and acknowledged. However, his body, facial expression, and affect quickly shifted to worry and depression. This weekend he was invited to an open house and predicted its outcome: "It's going to be the same damn thing as in my class. I'm going to feel incredibly inadequate and I won't say anything. I'll just withdraw and everyone will think I'm a boring, stupid jerk!" I was surprised by the sudden shift in his feelings about himself and his intense pessimism. Was he having a reaction to the progress he was making? That is, was he aggressively containing the grandiosity that got stirred by his social success? Did he need to undo his step forward? All hypotheses seemed valid.

I could have chosen an empathic interpretation of this pernicious defensive behavior. But given the shortness of time left in the session and knowing that such material was explored in detail before, I chose to address his state in a more directly cognitive-behavioral way. I used an empathic, soothing tone and said, "It sounds like you fully expect that you will behave just like a nerd who has nothing interesting to say and you're already dismal about it. It's interesting how you just described how confidently you socialized at the party. You can show a different, charming part of you and really enjoy it" (both the sense of mastery and narcissistic exhibitionism). He grudgingly agreed, "Yes, but you know what happens in my class and these are the same people." I replied, "It sounds like you're holding onto the expectation that you will fail socially here and that no one will want to spend time with you despite some recent success. It sounds like you may need to see yourself as a loser, like it's a part of your identity. Is that possible?" He replied, "My mother always wanted my older sister to do well so I couldn't." We went on to discuss how he felt trapped and stunted by these parental and older sibling expectations and his desire to free himself from them grew.

I returned to the present and suggested, "These same people are in both classes with you and in the second class you've described feeling good about your performance. Why not assume the party will be like how you are in your successful class?" He became curious about this possibility and decided it was time to allow for other possibilities rather than assume the absolute worst.

CHAPTER 4

DERIVATION OF
THE CURRENT MODEL

This book is an attempt to provide a useful model of empathic short-term psychotherapy. Guidelines will be suggested for undertaking this approach. However, this material ultimately needs to be integrated with therapists' creative thinking about how to help each unique client. We need to be willing to reexamine the ordinary, to challenge old theoretical assumptions, to question what really works for our clients and what works for us as clinicians. Creativity and flexibility are needed in conducting crisis intervention, brief therapy, or longer-term psychotherapy. Those two qualities are necessary not only to treat the patient but to sustain the psychological health of the clinician.

NEWER CONCEPTUAL METAPHORS
FOR BRIEF PSYCHOTHERAPY

In this spirit, let's take a fresh look at one of the very basic assumptions of psychoanalysis that is itself a system of hypothetical constructs. Freud used a nineteenth-century energy model, derived from the physics of his day, to understand, explain, and predict the workings of the psyche and human behavior. Although his model was and is quite useful in understanding the dynamics of the mind, it is based on a primarily linear model of causality. This model was associated with logical positivism, which was the prevailing philosophy of science of that day.

However, we are learning that much in nature operates nonlinearly or in many directions at once. And often in complex systems like human beings, the emergent whole becomes more than the sum of its parts, even if the parts are id, ego, and superego. Today, most clinicians acknowledge that despite all that we have studied about humans, on every level, it is still very difficult to predict a person's behavior at a given time because of the complexity of the human system. Is there some useful construct beyond that of psychodynamics?

Many therapists may be familiar with the concepts of dynamics and of systems as they are applied to psychodynamics and family systems. Going back to the basics, dynamics involves the study of how a system changes and the understanding of the forces that influence the behavior of that system. Thelen and Smith (1994) suggest that in natural systems, especially biological ones, increasing the forces affecting the system may result in sudden spurts of change in the behavior of the system. That change can be qualitatively different, or even new. Human beings are this kind of system.

There are newer models for understanding such systems and states of all kinds. These models attempt to address the complex phenomena of "parallel processing, bidirectional causality, and reverberating feedback that characterize both cognitive and social organizations" (McGuire 1973, p. 448), which I believe are also experienced in conducting psychotherapy. (This is especially so when looking at the interaction of transference and countertransference in a session and in looking at how clients grow.)

The models use such interrelated concepts as nonlinear dynamical systems theory, self-organization theory (Abraham et al. 1990), and chaos theory (Gleick 1987) and its latest form, complexity theory (Waldrop 1992). Having generated extensive interest in physics, biology, and chemistry, these concepts may offer a way of understanding change and growth in psychological systems as well (Barton 1994).

These ideas are starting to be used to study aspects of memory, sleep, learning processes, and infant development. On a higher level these concepts have been applied to theories of family and marital therapy, theories of mental states and their transitions, and the development of psychopathology. On a higher level yet, complexity theory has been used to understand the weather, as well as economic and political systems.

In the psychology arena these concepts may ultimately help explain better how human beings think, feel, and behave, and they may complement information provided by current models. Currently these theories are being applied to psychology in more of a qualitative, metaphorical fashion than in hard mathematical terms. Thelen and Smith (1994), however, use these concepts specifically to reanalyze infant research on behavior and cognition and perhaps to create a newer model of child development.

Self organization theory focuses on the process by which a structure or pattern may spontaneously emerge in an open system. That is, when sufficient energy is inputted to a system, it then attempts to order and organize itself into more and more complex structures without an external design. This new system behaves in complex yet ordered ways, resisting further perturbations. The emergent organization is totally different from the elements that constituted the original system. The patterns that the system now exhibits cannot be predicted solely from the features of its original elements.

In the human psyche arena we can see elements of this theory in the work of Sperry (1993), who is associated with the study of consciousness and the "cognitive psychology revolution." He developed a bidirectional theory about causality that had implications for all of science. He asserted that the neuronal activity of the brain leads to the emergence of mental states and other higher systems of consciousness. These mental states are inexplicably different from the original brain states. Once developed, these mental states can influence subsequent brain activity and behavior (Hergenhahn 1994).

Sampson (1994) took this theory one step further: "Not only are brain functions implicated in consciousness, and consciousness (as an emergent reality) in brain functions, but so too are sociohistorical functions implicated in the control of both consciousness and brain functions even as the latter are implicated in sociohistorical functions" (p. 818). Here is a theory integrating the roles of the environment, our biology, and our psychology in forming our psyches and vice versa. For example, Sampson's theory could account for the change in kinds of psychopathology that we see today instead of what Freud dealt with at the turn of the century, such as the growth in the diagnosis of narcissistic disorders.

Chaos theory is somewhat misnamed because it refers to a chaotic system that develops from deterministic rules. This theory describes the behavior of a system when it is in some way perturbed and how the dynamic behavior of that system leads to unpredictable change in the system over time. Scientists have found that the dynamics of these nonlinear and chaotic systems are unpredictable from their initial state, yet they do exhibit patterns over time. In addition, over time the system settles into a preferred mode of behavior. It is "attracted" to being in a particular state.

One of the implications of these theories for psychology is understanding that what we assume to be immutable phenomena or "human nature" may actually be our looking at a human system when it is in a certain state because certain internal and external conditions prevail. But if the system, such as the human mind, is disturbed and provided with some energy, we may see that same system change in possibly chaotic ways and then change into a different stable state. But even if a complex system is stable it will still have its minor fluctuations. When the fluctuations are strong enough and sustained enough they become "the source of new forms in behavior and development . . . that account for the nonlinearity of much of the natural world" (Thelen and Smith 1994, p. 63).

The chaotic concept of *sensitive dependence* (on initial conditions of a system), known popularly as the *butterfly effect*, may also be relevant to psychological systems. It refers, in part, to the notion that "initial, minor local events can serve to undermine predictability by sometimes significantly altering the course of future events" (Mandel 1995, p. 106). For example, such is the case when scientists say that a butterfly flapping its wings in one part of the world can ultimately cause a hurricane in another.

Bandura (1982), a cognitive-behaviorist, implied that the individual was an example of a sensitively dependent system. Mandel (1995) went on to integrate both concepts as possibly referring to the notion that events, whenever they occur, even if they seem trivial in a person's life, can have serious consequential effects on the trajectory the person's life will take, if those trivial events come at critical times.

Research using nonlinear dynamics concepts suggests that behavior is predictable within a certain range of conditions, and when the human system is disturbed behavior becomes unpredictable or settles into another pattern (Putnam 1988, Reidbord and Redington 1992). This may be another way of understanding development as well as the vicissitudes of psychopathology.

Both concepts of sensitive dependence and periodicity of behavior may also be useful in understanding and tracking the myriad states of mind or consciousness that people experience even during the course of one session. In turn, these concepts may illuminate the clinician's task of monitoring their interactions with the client.

Appreciating the plastic, dynamic nature of psychological functioning may also assist those therapists unaccustomed to working with more severely disturbed people. They may have a tendency to underestimate the full range of intactness and looseness (regression) of people's psyches in general and those of different diagnostic categories. There may also be a tendency to miss the subtle signs when a patient is starting to go into or come out of a disturbed psychological state.

While chaos theory has awakened us to the nonlinear patterns of human and other systems, complexity theory goes even further to explain the "structure, the coherence, the self-organizing cohesiveness of complex systems" (Waldorp 1992, p. 12). Ambitious in its scope, it is an attempt to illuminate the interconnections among all people and things in the universe. Complexity theory addresses the interrelationships among evolution, chaos, entropy, and order in all systems.

To extend the metaphor, I have used these concepts in thinking about the usefulness of conducting therapy as a meteorologist would track a hurricane using the newer, nonlinear approach. (This analogy was offered to me by Carlton E. Wynter, Ph.D., a population ecologist, in a personal communication.) That is, I try to appreciate that a human being, like a weather system, is a complex, self-organizing, system with unpredictable elements. A person is a complex system or set of systems that is very adaptable, is sensitive to internal and environmental conditions, and has chaotic and ordered aspects to its functioning. Like watching the startup of a hurricane, it is almost impossible to determine all the original conditions that caused the pathology/storm system the patient presents to us. And, even knowing all the original conditions will not make us certain about what that person/weather system will do the next moment. Therefore, as a hurricane tracker/therapist I try first to understand the patient's unique dynamics, watch and observe the impact of our interactions on the patient's self, and wait to bring in theoretical concepts that seem to best explain the phenomena we hear described. The more we track the patient/hurricane and test out theoretical concepts, the more accurate we become in our understanding of that system. We would then become more accurate in understanding what perturbations, that is, therapeutic interventions, would lead to stabilizing the human system. Of course, a human is much more complex than the weather. It is as if the theoretical model we construct with the client needs to be created and refined for each as we go along.

Let's come down from the stratosphere and see how this might be relevant to clinical theory and psychotherapy.

Using the New Metaphors within Self Psychology

Goldstein (in press) attempted to apply concepts of self organization and chaos theory to psychoanalytic theory with a focus on ego functions. Can these concepts apply to self psychology theory and clinical work? Kohutian theory does assume linear development in the psychological phenomena it describes. But aspects of several of its concepts do resonate with self organization and complexity theories. A first point of correspondence is Kohut's fundamental concept of the nuclear self and its development. The development of the nuclear self can be understood metaphorically as an example of self organization emerging from a complex system. Given the appropriate energy input, that is parental nurturance and attunement in addition to physical sustenance, the infant's psyche emerges. The infant now has a core self that is dynamically stable over time and space and has preferred states of being. In contrast to Freud's concept of the ego, the Kohutian self is not always interested in maintaining a static equilibrium and tension reduction, but is propelled toward mastery and growth. The Kohutian self may respond to random events by becoming disrupted or by "appropriating them," that is, using them to lay down structure and grow. One example might be the process of transmuting internalization.

Self psychology, with its emphasis on understanding what an event (intrapsychic or external) means for that patient's subjective experience and how it affects the patient's development, may actually be using a nonlinear way of understanding the patient's experience. Empathic introspection or making sense of a person's unique experience, how he internalizes things and weaves a narrative of his life, may represent a different, perhaps more open attitude of inquiry. Here the therapist does not presume linear cause and effect sequences in normal development or in the operations of defenses when the patient describes his life. In fact, linearity in our vicarious introspection might lead to an inaccurate and more incomplete picture of what the patient is experiencing.

In my adaptation of self psychology to brief therapy, I attempt to be open to the possibilities that the phenomena we are working to understand may not progress or regress as we assume. This model does not presume that people from varying cultures and socioeconomic classes follow the same path of personality and social development as those from a middle-class European culture. The therapist uses empathic inquiry to understand the client's unique development, the forces and important subjective symbols in the client's life. This therapeutic attitude may facilitate working with a wider variety and class of people more effectively, more humanely, and more respectfully.

Even the important role of insight as part of the cure in psychoanalysis can be seen in a different light if we perceive the patient as a dynamic system whose psyche is a set of dynamic structures and/or functions. The question is, should we solely pursue insight into their intrapsychic conflicts, or should we pursue an understanding of the dynamic interplay of their needs, perceptions, defenses, and actions? Should we not help the patient identify the mental state changes he experiences so that he can apprehend and work with them?

Likewise our empathic attunement to the patient is not a static, linear experience as it sometimes seems when therapists refer to transference–countertransference phenomena in a session. Rather, it is a dynamic, mutually resonating experience evoking reactions on many affective, cognitive, and even physiological levels in both participants.

While most dynamic clinicians agree that the phenomenon of transference exists, it is often described as the therapist's taking on aspects of, or selfobject functions of, an important person in the patient's life. The transference relationship is presumed to change over time. However, when more closely examined, transference reactions may change even within a session. Furthermore, anecdotal information from other clinicians adds to my impression that a client may have more than one transference reaction at the same time. For example, the patient may relate to the therapist as both an idealized and mirroring selfobject and oscillate between the two internal experiences. Let's return to clinical theory to see how creativity and flexibility were used to adapt self psychology to brief treatment.

EARLIER ATTEMPTS TO ADAPT SELF PSYCHOLOGY TO SHORTER-TERM THERAPY

Self psychology has had an impact on psychoanalysis in terms of how it reconceptualized healthy development, pathology, and approach to treatment. However, systematic applications of self psychology to shorter-term therapy are still relatively few in number. Historically, one may look to the work of Balint and colleagues (1972) who, along with Malan at the Tavistock Institute, developed "focal therapy." They worked on a shorter-term model of psychoanalytic psychotherapy that had some classical, object relations, and nascent self psychological aspects to it. The curative role of the relationship between therapist and patient was given some importance, as was the use of proto-selfobject supports to aid the patient between sessions.

The work was carried on by the Ornsteins (A. Ornstein 1986, P. Ornstein 1988, Ornstein and Ornstein 1972), who later became two of the prime explicators of Kohut and self psychology. The Ornsteins felt that dynamic therapy was a process, and that focal therapy was on the same continuum of psychoanalysis and psychoanalytic therapy since it used the same theory of personality, psychopathology, treatment, and theory of cure. Their model, later referred to as *psychoanalytic focal therapy*, will be discussed below.

Goldberg (1973) is also considered to have made one of the first formal attempts to apply emerging self psychological concepts (then referred to as narcissistic concepts) to shorter-term therapy. He had suggested the addition of a new diagnostic category of "acute narcissistic injuries" and a new treatment for it. This would later form the basis for his idea of a self psychologically informed psychotherapy rather than a psychoanalysis. The treatment centered around the therapist's providing needed narcissistic functions to the patient to restore the patient's narcissistic equilibrium. (We would now call those functions idealizing, mirroring, and twinship.) With that in place, underlying childhood narcissistic longings could be understood and addressed through interpretation.

Other efforts had been made to apply self psychology to a wider range of clients and to use shorter time frames. Lazarus (1982, 1988) used self psychological principles to conduct brief therapy with "narcissistically disturbed" people, including elderly patients. He also viewed short-term therapy as a way to restore the patient's self-esteem and sense of self, and restore functioning to a premorbid level. This would be accomplished by the therapist's provision of those needed selfobject functions to the patient. While he emphasized that the major utility of brief therapy was restoration of the patient's prior level of functioning, he did allow that therapy might lead to internalization of psychic structure and encourage insight and working through even after termination.

Chernus (1983) both delineated and enlarged the scope of the Ornsteins' focal therapy approach in detailing a case conducted by P. Ornstein. Within the Ornstein model of psychoanalytic focal therapy, the focal conflict, was defined as the circumscribed problem, which initially could be unconscious or preconscious. It was a result of a conflict or structural deficit in the patient and emerged into consciousness as a result of empathic listening in the treatment. A focal conflict was thought to be precipitated by a recent event that overwhelmed the person's psychological defenses.

In this approach the therapist selected clients using trial interpretations, assessed motivation for insight, and identified a focal issue. In treatment the therapist actively interpreted the transference using the triangle of insight. Efforts were made to understand why the patient's defense system could not contain or resolve the affects stirred by the current conflict. In the earlier stage of this model goals of focal therapy had involved defense analysis and conflict resolution. But now they included internalization of the therapist's (later to be called selfobject) functions and structure building of the self.

The work was confined to the focal conflict—that area of pathology that became reactivated in the treatment as a result of the empathic work. Part of the working-through process would involve looking at how patients now experienced their other current relationships besides the transferential relationship to the therapist. Treatment involved empathic interpretations of how the current stressors caused the focal problem and had an impact on the state of the patient's self. The meaning of particular symptoms and defenses was explored as possible attempts to maintain psychological equilibrium.

The major therapeutic approach would be to convey a sustained sense of understanding to the patient and then explain to him his particular self–selfobject dynamics that related to the focal conflict and underlying deficit. Chernus (1983) cited the Ornsteins' (1977) belief that "empathy, when used with careful attention to wording and timing, may promote the therapeutic process regardless of the nature and severity of psychopathology or length of treatment" (p. 220).

The current Ornstein model is fully explicated in formal self psychological concepts. It continues to be process rather than technique oriented. The therapist needs to convey her understanding of the client even before having a complete understanding of his dynamics. This understanding, however, is offered tentatively and in a more open-ended fashion. The Ornsteins also elaborate on how providing empathy is not simply reflecting what a patient feels but linking that material to thoughts, a particular event, and what happens afterward.

Elson (1986) employed self psychotherapy with patients of all ages and backgrounds. (Kohut held a seminar with Elson's university therapy staff.) Many of her cases were shorter term than traditional psychoanalysis and psychotherapy.

Gardner (1991) adapted self psychology to formal, time-limited therapy in a community mental health center setting. Consistent with Chernus and Elson, she demonstrated that this approach could restore a client to a premorbid level of functioning and begin the process of structure building. In her approach the therapist establishes a self–selfobject bond with the client. As a result of the explicit articulation and acceptance of the client's selfobject needs, the client's self starts to repair. Consequently, the client is then able to recruit new internal and external resources into his self–selfobject environment with which to pursue his life.

Baker (1991) has also developed a model for applying self psychology to shorter-term therapy. He delimits its usefulness to those who do not have severe psychopathology. He views this brief version of self psychology mostly as a way to restore functioning and serve as a palliative for those with severe self pathology. In his model one notes increased importance placed on perceptions, images, and "sustaining selfobject memories" (p. 301), that is, cognitive factors, along with a major emphasis on affective experience in treating the patient.

Alpert (1992) and his group at the Short-Term Dynamic Psychotherapy Institute adapted aspects of self psychology to their approach. This group originally employed Davanloo's approach to brief therapy, but moved to a nonconfrontational, empathic posture that they found produced more effective, perhaps longer-lasting results. It is an active form of brief therapy that concentrates treatment on the pathological impact of loss and separation for the individual. In the most systematic way to date, they demonstrated the greater success of the provision of an empathic holding environment in deeply helping clients than of the confronting, dynamic approach of Davanloo.

KEY ASPECTS OF THE EMPATHIC BRIEF PSYCHOTHERAPY MODEL

My model is consistent with aspects of all those cited above. The current model, however, expands the focal approach in several ways. In self psychology, empathy was first thought to be a data-gathering tool and only later identified as being curative. In the current model, empathy and empathic listening are systematic, central parts of the treatment strategy. The focal issue is now considered to be any recurring cluster of affective, cognitive, or behavioral symptoms that the patient presents, which is a manifestation of an underlying self vulnerability.

Like the approach of Lichtenberg and colleagues (1992), in my approach sexuality and aggression are no longer seen as the basic drives of the psyche. But, in a departure from earlier self psychologists, "pathological" aspects of sexuality and aggression aren't always viewed as merely breakdown products of the self (for example, aggression can foster individuation). The reader will see a shift away from interpretations based on linear dynamics of impulse-defense or need-frustration to ones based on patterns of important selfobject experiences and their linked interpersonal themes aimed at restoring or promoting the self. Attempts will be made to involve the three interacting dimensions of affect/motivation, cognition, and behavior.

The therapy experience is a more active one for both participants than in a pure self psychological approach. The patient is continuously asked to explore, be curious about himself, convey his experiences, and work on hypotheses about himself with the therapist. This includes how he experiences his body and psyche in the moment, that is, self states. The therapist is likely to be more active both in terms of offering interpretations and in providing psychoeducation. In addition, I follow the path of optimal responsiveness to the client's selfobject needs rather than pure interpretation of selfobject needs or optimal frustration of the client's needs.

I agree with the self psychological clinicians cited that while the therapy relationship is the major curative factor, the analysis of the transference between therapist and patient remains in the background. Much of the working-through process is done around interpretations of the patient's other relationships in his self–selfobject milieu. The therapy relationship is brought in to illuminate the dynamics in these other relationships or when a negative therapeutic current is detected. The working-through process continues after the therapy is ended.

While acceptance of the patient, understanding, and explaining are still the foundation of the treatment, what is understood and explained encompasses the three linked spheres of psychological functioning (affective, cognitive, behavioral) including the verbal and nonverbal realms. When successful, the client's experience of feeling understood by the therapist has a reverberating, multidimensional effect, both mentally and physically.

The experience of feeling understood deeply and in a sustained way leads to a greater sense of cohesion, continuity, and vitality of the self. In this different psychological and physical place the client is better able to start dealing with overwhelming affective states, to better organize his thoughts in order to problem solve and modify his expectations of his self and other, and to act in the interpersonal world to get his needs met. The sustained use of acceptance, understanding, and explaining leads to the consolidation of the patient's self, which allows for the possibility of deeper work. Thus, this approach is more than just supportive and can initiate the process of structure building.

The therapist does offer explanations to the patient of the focal issue by making self–selfobject interpretations using that same triangular transferential perspective (patient to past figure, patient to present figures, patient to therapist). Explaining the patient's psychodynamics in terms of the origin of his selfobject needs, defenses, and consequent behaviors enlarges the impact of the therapy experience and grounds it in a developmental perspective.

The patient begins to use the therapist as a selfobject who may provide the functions of containing, soothing, organizing, cohesion building, mirroring, and self-esteem enhancing. In addition, the therapist educates the patient about relevant aspects of human development, psychodynamics, and psychopathology. In the current model the therapist explicitly talks about and trains the patient to be empathically curious about her patterns of affect, cognition, and behavior, and how they feed back to each other. The therapist and patient look at how the patterns shift when in different mental states, and they try to identify what self–selfobject responsiveness causes a positive shift in self state and what failures initiate a shift into a negative self state.

The patient gains a deeper understanding of the specific psychological issue and what it takes to sustain or enable the self to grow around that focal issue. When the patient understands his needs better and why he employs the defense pattern that he uses, he is then freer to recruit more productive methods. Also, as a result of understanding his needs and his reactions when they are not met, the client is then better able to prevent those situations from happening in the same way or to minimize their negative impact. Technically speaking, selfobject responsiveness from the therapist and others leads to enhanced self functioning and structure. The client may now be able to fill in some psychological deficit and even resume growth.

What Is Curative in Empathic Brief Psychotherapy?

Historically, cure was originally thought to be accomplished through resolution of conflict between drives, then by replacing id with ego, or by replacing a rigid superego with a benign one. Next, cure was seen as the development of insight. Kohut originally defined cure in terms of the buildup of the structure of the self through transmuting internalization of the therapist's functions via interpretation and working through of the selfobject transferences. But by the time he wrote *How Does Analysis Cure?* (1984), he subordinated all the other elements in a cure to the higher goal of the patient embedding himself, over time, in an environment of self–

selfobject relationships that would nourish him. This last definition of cure fits with what brief self psychotherapy can begin to set in motion, that is, validation of and an awareness of one's selfobject needs, a strengthening of the self, and a reaching out to appropriate others to get response to developmentally appropriate needs.

COGNITIVE-BEHAVIORAL INTEGRATION WITHIN A SELF PSYCHOLOGY MODEL

It may seem as if I depart from other self psychologists when I don't give affective experience the exclusive focus. However, the cognitive aspect of one's psychological experience (i.e., thoughts and expectations), has always been an integral part of dynamic therapy. Likewise, linkages of the client's inner experience to her behavior have also been integral to therapy. The current model emphasizes the need to refer to all three spheres of functioning systematically when trying to understand the client and make interventions.

Michael Basch (1980, 1988), a psychoanalyst, theoretician, and affiliate of the school of self psychology, may have also provided some theoretical bridges between the psychodynamic and cognitive-behavioral, and perhaps neurological, realms. He defines the self as dealing with both affective and cognitive activities. He views affect as the wellspring of motivation. Cognition and information processing are thought to organize and maintain the affective system. Competence and self-esteem are considered the main motivations of human behavior. Consequently, he believes the main role of the therapist is to address the client's problem-solving capacity.

Martin (1993) attempts a theoretical integration between self psychology and cognitive therapy that is facilitated partly by Basch's work. He theorizes that sustained empathic failure during development leads to dysfunctional beliefs about one's self (concept) and to negative transferential relationships to others. In his version of brief therapy, structure building is out of the question. It needs to be substituted for by cognitive skill development that would help modify the distorted thoughts and beliefs that maintain dysfunctional interpersonal patterns. In his theoretical system the selfobject transferences are central in the assessment of the client but remain in the background of the primarily cognitively oriented treatment.

I believe that understanding and working with the client's selfobject relationships, both inside and especially those outside the therapy session, are essential not only for assessment but for treatment of the client. I agree, however, with Martin that the therapist does serve as a selfobject who helps enhance the self-esteem of the client and works on the client's dysfunctional thoughts and expectations. The therapist also educates the client about his selfobject needs and where to locate productive self–selfobject relationships. Yet, I believe that performing these roles requires addressing core affective experience, and then looking at the cognitive processes that mediate and inform the client's affect and behavior.

INFORMAL CASE PRESENTATION

The following case material is offered to give a sample of how the startup of an empathic brief psychotherapy case might be experienced. In the next chapter the structure of this approach will be articulated in greater technical detail. The treatment lasted nine sessions. This section demonstrates the provision of empathic understanding around a specific dilemma, which also illuminates the focal, underlying issue. The reader may observe that the therapist is fairly active and integrates some cognitive-behavioral elements in the session.

> Samantha, a 35-year-old architect, came for help in dealing with anxiety in the workplace, which she felt inhibited the quality of her work. She assertively requested short-term work because that was all the time she was prepared to give up from her busy day and evening schedule. She described having two prior therapy experiences totaling one year in duration that produced only a few positive results. Now she came partly because her lover felt that Samantha's intense anxiety left Samantha unable to take in her lover's help.
>
> Samantha started each session with her focus on her difficulties at work and then we would move to the underlying, intrapsychic focal issue. At work she described terrible anxiety anticipating making a presentation, which kept her up most of the night. Sometimes her mate could soothe her but increasingly less so. After the presentation she would feel crushed by the disappointment and shame she experienced in her own imperfect performance as well as envy of more competent colleagues. She believed that she did not win enough of her accounts. During the presentations she experienced herself as too passive and inhibited, not aggressive enough on behalf of her firm. At those times she allowed herself very little consolation from her important selfobjects. Objective positive feedback from her clients, colleagues, and bosses also did little to assuage her negative evaluation of herself.

In the first few sessions as I began to wonder what the focal self issue was underlying her work anxiety, I picked up on her anxious and somewhat demoralized mood. I suggested to her that she seems really disappointed in herself for needing to reach out to another for help again. She flushed, stared hard at me, and lowered her head, sadly agreeing. The long look she gave me indicated the possibility that she was also angry at needing help with her anxiety and perhaps angry at her lover for pushing her to come. I offered this trial interpretation: "I wonder if when you feel you let yourself down it makes you angry at yourself and you feel less worthy. And perhaps this attitude towards yourself gets compounded by the bad feeling that your partner told you to come, that she could do no more." Samantha nodded in agreement and added, "I feel that she gave up on me so she referred me to a therapist."

We then talked about what it was like for her at work and at home with her lover. Silently I began to hypothesize a dynamic link between the client's need to behave perfectly in order to deserve and maintain her ties to needed selfobjects and other objects. When she would experience herself as imperfect or failing, regardless of whether or not it was visible to others, she might feel her internal and external relations to important others were threatened.

The next two sessions focused on the links between external triggers to fears of failure that threatened her selfobject relationships and her expectations and defensive reactions. She became aware that when she felt disappointed in herself and the threat of psychic abandonment returned, she would withdraw from her partner and others. She would desperately want to be soothed and reassured but felt she could not ask for it. The other person had to identify her distress and provide a precisely attuned response.

It was in the third session that Samantha reported less anxiety and deflation as a result of her presentations. But she thought it was partly due to the presentations being less frequent. We talked about the need to help her sustain her gains now and after therapy ended.

Now that Samantha's interest was piqued about her self we looked at the genetic derivatives of her perfectionism and her need to show her parents that she was completely autonomous. She became aware that she couldn't ask for help or further training at work especially since her parents/authority figures were usually perceived as too fragile and overburdened. She seems to need to be mirrored by idealizable figures who will affirm her competencies and help contain her anxious and depressive reactions. But she seems only to have had failed idealizable figures. In compensation she turned to friends and to her partner as a twin who could commiserate and share her imperfections, which helped her to feel less bad but did not improve her performance.

Increasingly I discerned some transference to me as a containing figure who accepted her struggle with her anxiety as a legitimate area to be addressed. I suggested concrete things she could try to break into her negative work cycle. These included ways to manage her distressing affects and countering distorted thoughts in the moment. Affect management was enhanced by first empathically trying to understand the pattern of what it felt like when she experienced a work failure. We came up with the idea that when she felt distressed, she should take a few minutes out, no matter how urgent work might be at the time, and try to figure out how she was feeling and give some validity to her reactions. There was probably something happening at work that was stirring up that same old self state. She would then be better able to differentiate transferential reactions from her other reactions so that later she could use that information to respond in a more effective way. She was willing to try this inner exploration, although she admitted that it was unsettling to get in touch with her self.

In the next chapter guidelines for actually conducting the therapy and case examples from each phase of treatment will be presented. We'll return to Samantha's case there.

EMPATHIC BRIEF PSYCHOTHERAPY WITH INDIVIDUALS

BEGINNING EMPATHIC SHORT-TERM THERAPY

The initial therapeutic contact begins with the first telephone interchange. The beginning sessions then set the overall structure for the rest of the therapy experience. For experienced therapists the pace may seem quicker, more intense, and require more affective and cognitive activity from both therapist and client. However, once under way, the self psychological therapy sessions become more fluid and varied in pace and depth.

The therapist's first goal, as always, is to establish rapport with the client and begin to discern what selfobject functions the therapist may need to offer the client. The therapist suggests what would be useful to cover in the first meeting, such as getting acquainted and what difficulties and goals the client wants to work on.

As part of that process it's helpful to inquire how the client feels about coming for treatment. Expectations of what the experience will be like, the client's anticipated length of treatment, and negative feelings about coming are especially important to identify and understand. If I sense strong reservations about being in therapy, I then may explore fears of dependency, shame and anger responses to needing help, fears of having one's emotional life churned up only to be disappointed by the therapist, and reactions to the short-term nature of the therapy. Not only does this inquiry facilitate the therapeutic alliance, but it enables the therapist to quickly address potential client resistances. If the client voices such negative concerns, the therapist explores further and empathically reframes these reservations as understandable self-protective reactions. The therapy process is now off and running.

The client is asked to talk about the problems and goals for which help is being sought. The therapist particularly wants to know why the client is seeking help now and how the problems had been dealt with in the past. The therapist may then ask the client to prioritize the issues.

The therapist begins to grasp the client's pattern of how he protects and preserves his self, that is, his defensive and healthy adaptive patterns. Both client and therapist begin to look for and make explicit the links between the client's affective reactions, his expectations of self and others, and subsequent behaviors. The therapist wants to hear about the patient's selfobject milieu while growing up, and the narrative the client constructed of his life.

The tone of the therapist's questions should convey a genuine interest and curiosity about the client's struggles. The inquiry is directed toward understanding the meaning of the client's experiences rather than simply judging or labeling them. In so doing the therapist begins to model empathic introspection, which the client can employ himself later. This serves as a way of exploring himself and as a model of attunement.

The therapist is inwardly assessing the client in terms of general psychological functioning and self functioning. The assessment should include a clear identification of the client's strengths and resources. The therapist switches to more of a formal mental status dialogue when serious pathology or threat to the client is expressed or suspected. The therapist uses her own inner reactions to what the client says and does to guide her inquiry.

Self-State Assessment

The client's self state is monitored every session and guides the therapist toward the focal issues. It goes beyond the general assessment of the patient's functioning and mental status. It is an intimate attempt to understand how the patient experiences his self and the world in the moment. Through the verbal and nonverbal sharing during the session, the therapist is trying to discern how cohesive or how fragmented the patient's self is, how stable and continuous the patient experiences his self, and how vitalized or how depleted his self appears to be. The therapist is also trying to establish what resources and patterns of defenses the client uses to maintain his self.

Some self psychologically oriented therapists assume that a cohesive self is characteristic of the normal-neurotic individual, the chronically depleted self is characteristic of those with depressions, and the chronically fragmented self is characteristic of those with borderline conditions, multiple personality disorders, some narcissistic disorders, posttraumatic stress disorder (PTSD), and psychoses. I agree with Stolorow and colleagues' (1987) proposal that psychopathology of the self resulting from disruptions may be on a severity continuum where the variables considered are the vitality, cohesiveness, and continuity of the self over time. The self structure of the client is also assessed as the selfobject transference develops.

In the session the therapist looks for the patterned way that the client presents himself and experiences himself in the therapy milieu. There will cluster together a particular way that the client attends, thinks, feels, perceives, remembers, talks, and interacts with the therapist. His clothing and even posture may be slightly different in a different self state so as to form a different gestalt of his being.

The therapist needs to be attentive to these state changes so as to know when she is being optimally responsive and enhancing the client's self. She also needs to be aware when the client is feeling discontinuous or getting fragmented or depleted as a result of what is going on in or outside the session, and to address it promptly.

In a self psychological assessment we go beyond asking about the presenting complaints and their history and how the client coped with the problems. We want to know the quality of the selfobject milieu within which he currently functions. Focusing around the key difficulties identified, we ask about who and what enable him to cope, who and what motivate him to be expansive, and who and what cause him to weaken and become more symptomatic. Following this line of inquiry (Ringstrom 1994b), the therapist is informed in three important ways: (1) it gives the therapist some idea of the client's current level of selfobject relatedness, (2) it gives feedback on the ways in which the client has recruited other people to help restore self cohesion, continuity, vitality, self-esteem, and a positive self concept, and (3) it suggests who may be recruited to provide those selfobject experiences. The therapist uses that information about other selfobject relationships to compare how the client responds to the therapist's effort to help in terms of being restorative versus being angering, depleting, shaming, or fragmenting. It is especially important to know the dimensions of the client's selfobject relatedness when the brief therapist empathically but actively explores the disturbing focal patterns and articulates the client's selfobject longings.

Establishing the Focus of Treatment

The therapist begins to summarize and synthesize her understanding of what the client is struggling with and what the client wants. That understanding is conveyed to the client, who is then asked to modify or elaborate on what is said. The therapist also begins to offer trial interpretations of possible underlying issues in these first sessions. They may be presented as clarifications or explanations of the dynamics underlying one of the presenting complaints. The focus of treatment begins to crystallize in the mind of the therapist.

In general, the focus of treatment is on the recurring pattern that leads to the distress and destabilization of the client. The focal issue typically relates to the underlying, chronic lack of selfobject responsiveness on the part of the client's environment, which leads to negative self states and other sequelae in the vulnerable self. The presenting complaints are manifestations of these dynamics. The client's attempts to contain these negative states are then addressed. Those that assist his stability are noted and may be encouraged, while those that compound his difficulties are worked on in treatment. The psychodynamics underlying the precipitating events are linked up to the pattern of selfobject failure in the client's childhood. Their impact on current relationships is linked as in the triangle of insight.

In brief therapy, one needs to start with a focal issue for several reasons. If no focus is identified, the result may be a confused, diffused therapy with no salient issue ever worked through. The focus helps to contain the intensity of the transference and countertransference as well as regression in brief therapy. In addition, managed care requires the accountability that a focused treatment plan facilitates. If the client responds poorly to the treatment, then the therapist needs to reassess what is going on. Is the client not being helped or is the therapist having difficulty being persistent in the focus because of the tension it incurs? The most helpful focus needs to be identified anew and the objectives and goals of therapy readjusted.

The first session ends with a discussion of fees, insurance, and attendance, provisions for the client in case of crises, and confidentiality. This is especially important if the case is reviewed by others or the client is asked to fill out diagnostic questionnaires. The therapist suggests the client think about how the session went, what may have been learned, and the goals for the therapy in light of the first session. The therapist indicates that she will also think over the session and begin to formulate the best way to help and how long she estimates it will take.

Between the first few sessions the therapist is formulating the nature and degree of the client's pathology and strengths, identifying the specific focal issue(s) to be worked on, outlining the treatment plan for the focal issue(s), and estimating length of treatment. To make these decisions the therapist incorporates the information received from the client with impressions of how well she and the client interacted over the course of the session.

The number of focal goals to be worked on needs to be realistically determined and probably limited to two different areas. This is especially necessary when the session limit is predetermined. But keep in mind that working on particular content areas is only part of the way the therapist assists the client. The other part of the treatment is how the attuned therapist provides consolidating, mirroring, and organizing functions that start to get internalized in the client. From the first call the therapist is already helping the client identify his selfobject needs and validate them. This attunement plays a powerful nonspecific role in helping to start the healing and growing process in the client.

Finding and maintaining a focus of treatment (a.k.a. focal adherence) is a challenge. In self psychology this implies deeply listening to the client, understanding what is important for the client to work on, and being responsive in the time allotted. Characteristics of the client himself affects how smoothly this process will go. For example, Hoglend and Piper (1995) suggest that clients with good object relations will have a more successful treatment if the focus is consistently maintained. Those with poor object relations actually do better if the therapist is more flexible in maintaining the focus and provides more of a holding environment. They suggest that dependent clients or those with problems of trust who were treated in a less focused way showed "improved morale, gradually improved adaptation after therapy, and probably positive responses from significant others, which would serve to reinforce changes started in therapy" (p. 626).

In the second session the therapist inquires how the client experienced the first session. Often clients have a neutral to mildly positive response and have some hope of improvement in their situation. Negative reactions need to be explored. They may mask possible signs of anxieties (due to dread of reexperiencing disappointment in treatment), narcissistic injury, or lack of motivation for treatment.

The therapist outlines her understanding of the client's difficulties on a level the client will comprehend. The therapist explains the linkage between the precipitating events and the relevant psychodynamic of the client. The therapist suggests the focus of treatment and the best way to help. The client is encouraged to respond and fine-tune the plans.

In the following sessions the therapist and client make the linkages between the client's experience of having his needs responded to and their positive impact on his sense of self, between needs not being responded to and their negative impact on his self (self-esteem, self concept, expectations, state of his self) and behavior, and between patterns developed with parental selfobject relationships and current relationships.

Identifying Clients Who May Terminate Early

Clients may drop out of treatment because of variables specifically related to the clients themselves, to the relationship between client and therapist, or to factors related to the specific therapist. While findings are not yet conclusive, some research on which clients drop out of treatment suggest the following client profile: these clients come more often from the lower socioeconomic classes, have had little exposure to the mental health field, and are psychologically unsophisticated. As a result they tend to expect advice that will fix their problems rather than seeing it as an active, collaborative effort. Borderline personalities seem to be a prominent diagnostic category in this group. Of course, this leaves out the possible negative contribution of cultural, racial, age, and sexual biases, the role of therapy orientation, and poor matching between client and therapist.

Strupp and Hadley (1979) have been studying therapy outcome and therapist factors related to outcome for many years. The findings of Strupp's current research offer useful thoughts for the clinician. Using a case study format, Strupp and colleagues (1992) found that client dropout was related to the therapist not listening empathically, not having a clear focus for the therapeutic dialogue, seeming to criticize the client, and overlooking parts of the preliminary clinical agenda such as history taking.

Psychological Detectives

During the beginning of brief treatment I try to engage the client in becoming a psychological detective, that is, taking a curious, empathic attitude about himself. When I can, I try to make it playful. I encourage an open, creative attitude. Together we generate hypotheses or hunches rather than my giving the client interpretations. The client draws on his experiences. The therapist draws on her own personal experiences, training, and clinical experiences.

The hypotheses are initially formed around selfobject dynamics where

I relate early selfobject experiences to present experiences and to the trans-ference relationships. I encourage the client to construct the hypotheses in as vivid a way as possible using many sense modalities.

Very modest, doable assignments or advice are given. They are meant to test out our hypotheses about a pattern related to the focal issue and to be therapeutic. We learn from the client's reaction to doing it, and the assignment may help him. If it doesn't, we stop it. Assignments ultimately provide a safer place for the client to experience himself differently and motivate him to change.

CASE MATERIAL FROM THE BEGINNING PHASE OF EMPATHIC BRIEF THERAPY

Philippe: The First Sessions

Philippe, a chipper, thin, and stylish European man, decided to seek therapy at the suggestion of a woman whom he had just begun to date. In a relaxed and confident manner, he admitted that his friends had urged him to start treatment a year ago. His fiancée, Selena, had suddenly abandoned him and their jointly formed company, leaving him terribly distraught and depressed. Now he felt he wanted some assistance regarding this situation even though he had made progress and only thought of her "a few times a day rather than all the time." (Therapists have long noted the paradox that many people enter therapy when they start to feel better, perhaps because they feel better about themselves or they are strong enough to face their issues and try to change. They may also begin around anniversaries or developmental milestones such as marriage, the birth of a child, etc.)

He cheerfully declared, "I am just about to turn 40 next week, and I'm facing a midlife crisis." I nonverbally mirrored the import of his statement, wondered internally about his cheery attitude, and then asked how he felt he was in a crisis. He knew that he was entering the prime of his life but was blocked.

He felt he was a very creative person, loved working in furniture de-sign, but could never sustain his work goals and be the financial success and respected figure he wanted to be. He described himself currently as a supersalesman at an elite antique dealer. He felt he was painfully under-achieving. He believed himself to be dyslexic. In addition he was worried that he might have a problem with women since all his relationships with them seemed to fall apart despite his efforts and he did not want to be alone.

My first impression was that the goals for his short-term therapy seemed clear, that is, to help mourn the loss of his relationship to Selena, and to outline and begin to address possible issues around intimacy and career success. We would prioritize these goals a little later. However, my efforts to track and assess the state of his self during our initial meeting suggested there was more to be understood.

There was a physical intensity, drama, and pressure in his need to explain himself to me that came in waves. His self-esteem seemed to inflate and deflate rapidly as he described the events of the past five years of his life. The more distressing his tales of betrayal and abandonment by others, the more he wandered in his cognitive focus. His manicky qualities initially made me reverberate a little with anxious worry as to the cohesiveness of his self. Were these manic qualities signaling a tendency for his self to fragment?

My fatigue in trying to track the state of his self and the subtle incongruencies between his inflated self concept and distressed affect left me questioning the real goals. I began to feel a countertransferential pull to soothe him and visualized my physically containing him, partly to preserve myself as well. Concern about Philippe's potential hypomanic defense or more serious pathology made me decide that a fairly thorough psychological assessment was warranted at this point.

I introduced this impending change in the rhythm of the session from one of narrative flow to interview by changing my posture and summarizing what he had shared thus far. I employed a muted version of his affective tone to convey my understanding and to filter some of his tension. He seemed pleased that I understood his frustrations over his thwarted growth and his relationship concerns.

I indicated that to be thorough I wanted to make sure that I fully understood the nature of his difficulties and needed to ask him some questions. He readied himself and I then went through my mental status questions attempting to rule out major disorders, substance abuse, dyslexia, and attention deficit/hyperactivity disorder (ADHD). He revealed that he had been dependent on cocaine and alcohol for several years, but with some assistance of self-help groups he had been in recovery for the past five years. He did feel that he had a tendency to become addicted to substances such as caffeine and sweets but fought against that attraction.

Given the patient's tendency at times to behaviorally enact his inner difficulties and his trouble in relationships, I delicately explored his sexual identity and orientation. He declared he was enthralled by women and was not troubled by a sexual identity issue. However, occasionally he would have fantasies of being with men after a series of failed courtships with women but wouldn't act on them.

Although hypomanic at times, his symptoms and childhood history did not meet the formal criteria of ADHD disorder. If he had a form of this disorder, he had now developed compensatory devices. He was somewhat dyslexic but quite bright and creative. In addition, he appeared to manifest symptoms of anxiety and moderate episodic depression, and many symptoms consistent with a narcissistic personality disorder. Doing this assessment provided some structure and guidelines for me and was also necessary for record keeping and third-party reimbursement. However, I needed to go deeper, to reconnect with the state of his self to identify the focus of treatment.

At the end of the first session I continued to feel that he needed help in integrating and organizing what we had done together so that he could take it home with him and think about it. I summarized the tentative goals as he identified them and suggested that we continue delving into the psychological puzzles of his unsatisfactory relationships and careers.

He seemed to need to use me as a selfobject to help him contain his affective reactions, which would then enable him to synthesize new thinking about himself. This was later manifested in his request to tape record and listen to the sessions.

In the second session Philippe was still cheery. We discussed how he experienced his first therapy session. He indicated with some importance that he liked it and hoped it would be helpful but wanted to get on with it. I decided to return to the assessment not only to flesh out his presenting complaints but also to get a fuller view of the strengths and weaknesses that he would bring to our therapy venture.

While he indicated that neither he nor his family had any formal psychiatric history, he did experience some part of his self as continually being somewhat depressed. He said that this depressive underlayer would be present even during moments of happiness and he did not understand why. It was very easy for him to shift from an experience of triumph or joy to empty despair. He could then fantasize killing himself "the old fashioned way" by slitting his wrists in a bathtub bestrewn with lovely smelling flowers, candles, and his favorite music. In probing further, he indicated that he would never go through with it because life was such an interesting adventure.

I asked if this shifting was happening in his therapy as well. At first Philippe emphatically felt it did not, but then he wondered if a recent experience was an example of this. He explained that right before coming to our session today he was happy and looking forward to it in a hopeful way. Yet he found himself waiting for his session on a park bench and beginning to feel despair. This felt familiar but puzzling to him since he could never explain the shift. I responded by acknowledging his upset and indicating that it sounded like a sad and confusing place for him to be. I suggested that perhaps he couldn't hold on to the hopeful feelings about therapy since he had experienced so much disappointment in people and perhaps he was anticipating that the sessions would cause him to reexperience too much upset.

I then took a chance of trying to reframe and explain his negative reaction as a defense meant to preserve his self. "In fact," I said, "as strange as it seems, the despair might be serving two purposes: it might be a kind of anticipatory response to your therapy failing in the future, where you fear either I would fail you or you would mess it up. And, your despair might also start out as an attempt at managing the agitation you feel at getting your hopes raised." "You mean, I might be feeling depressed as a way to balance out my getting too excited?" Philippe asked. I indicated that I thought these ideas, though complex, were worth investigating.

I suggested that he begin to explore these hypotheses on his own by trying to become more aware of the chain of his reactions to whatever he experienced. We were looking for patterns to corroborate the hunches regarding his dynamics. I knew that Philippe used to practice meditation and understood how to turn his focus to his inner life. I indicated that he might not be able to sustain this introspective stance too long at first, but I assured him that his attention span would increase over time (as affect regulation improved).

I asked Philippe who seemed to be most helpful to him when he was struggling and who was least helpful. I asked these questions for two purposes: to gain a sense of his selfobject relatedness and predictions for the transference and to address the depressive states he got into when on his own. Unfortunately, he felt his former girlfriend, Selena, was his true friend. What helped him feel better was the possibility of hooking up with a new Selena or diverting himself with new social and work projects. I judged that he was not truly suicidal. However, I wanted to help him build a richer self–selfobject environment to sustain and stabilize him. Until then I hoped he could begin to rely on his therapy for that purpose. His taping the sessions and listening to them seemed to help stabilize him between our meetings.

Understanding and explaining is one of the fundamental tenets of doing self psychological therapy. In addition, my aim in this phase was to evaluate his receptivity to my offering some selfobject functions. I might be serving the purposes of affect management—both soothing and inspiring hope as an antidote to deflation—and organization of his thoughts and feelings. It was also a way to assess his psychological mindedness and ability to work with interpretations. In this situation I offered a sophisticated set of interpretations of his despair as a response to impending deflation and despair as a form of affect regulation and defense. He understood some of what I said and did work with it. I felt that I was probably close to addressing him on an appropriate psychological level but needed to convey the interpretations on a less abstract, intellectualized level.

After each of the three sessions I reviewed my understanding of his difficulties and goals. His physical intensity and activity level in the first sessions seemed to parallel the anxiety he felt at not being able to experience himself as competent and talented and as special as he needed to be. I began to hypothesize that grandiosity or, as Kohut termed it, "hypercathexis of the grandiose self" was a major defense he employed to ward off disappointment and angry frustrations. When this defense was unsuccessful it would lead to his feeling alternately as if he was flying apart or emptied out. He would then experience his self as both fragmenting and then deflating.

Ulman and Paul (1990) delineate a similar set of dynamics in their self psychological model of addictive personalities. They describe how a person may be addicted to an archaic selfobject that provided an altered self-experience involving "narcissistic fantasies and moods of narcissistic bliss" (p. 129). This selfobject could be a substance, a behavior, or a relationship to another person. The fantasies symbolically involve archaic experiences of either mirroring by another, idealizing, or twinship.

Philippe seemed to manifest a more complex dynamic where he would experience both a manic-like response to impending self fragmentation and a depressive one to an impending self deflation. In this situation Selena, the selfobject, was used to provide both antianxiety and antidepressive effects. Ulman and Paul define this addictive self disorder as one in which the person oscillates between a dissociative state in which he is merged with an idealized figure and one in which he is merged with an object who perfectly mirrors his exhibited grandiosity. The oscillation between these two states of mind creates the feeling of well-being in the person.

While Philippe was not currently a substance abuser, he perceived himself as compulsive and easily addicted to caffeine, chocolate, nicotine, alcohol, and other drugs. He referred to a penchant for mild sadomasochistic sex as well. He was able to wean himself periodically from these compulsive behaviors. However, how he used these substances and sadomasochistic sex to regulate his internal state and preserve his self seemed similar to Ulman and Paul's profile.

Philippe's Third Session

Although I now had some understanding of the dynamics of the state of his self, I needed the background on Philippe's early development in order to define his focal self issues. For example, how did early parental relationships affect who he chose now in a self-defeating way? He dramatically described how his family came from very poor French stock. His father landed in a distinguished army regiment and parlayed his connections there into future work opportunities. Philippe referred to his father as a gruff, insensitive alcoholic. He was a very lively fellow who spent most of his free time in the cafés. When he came home he would fill his wife and children with all his ideas for get-rich-quick schemes that they could implement. Philippe would always get excited by the possibility of his and his father's succeeding. Each time he realized that his father wasn't even going to act on the idea, Philippe would become deflated. His father would then make fun of him for believing he (Philippe) could succeed, too. Shame was added to the rage at his father's chronically disappointing him.

Rather than focus on his own work success, his father promoted his wife, who was a talented costume jewelry designer. He would demand that she create very elegant jewelry pieces for his suits to show off to his former, now successful, comrades in arms. In the retelling, Philippe began to believe that he might be replaying his father's "Rasputin" style of exploiting women, which distressed him.

Philippe then bitterly related that it was literally by his mother's hand that the family rose out of poverty into the middle class. He portrayed his mother as a very hard-working, obese woman with little self-confidence. While he felt loved by her, he experienced her as weak and ineffectual at home; she attended very little to him and his younger sister and brother.

His father seemed to expect great things from his firstborn son, but Philippe soon showed difficulty in learning to read and write. While he was verbally quite articulate, that channel was not open to him much in school. His father punished him for his dismal performance and Philippe began to deal with this source of shame and frustration by becoming contemptuous of most authority figures and rebelling at school. Consequently, he cut his education short and became unruly at home.

Philippe very much wanted to be mirrored by his parents, but was unable to perform in the traditional ways to obtain this mirroring from them. His mother gladly responded to his need for bodily admiration by dressing him up in the finest clothes. However, Philippe viewed his mother as fragile and depressed. To be mirrored by her was at first stimulating and then an empty experience as he witnessed her return to her depressive state. His father's tales of grandeur overstimulated his fantasies and left him to modulate them as well as deal with his de-idealization of his father. His parents were unable to provide the setting in which he could internalize ways of managing his overpowering thoughts and feelings.

Philippe had great difficulty transforming his childhood narcissistic yearnings into healthy self structure and functions. As a further consequence, his yearnings and fantasies never became metabolized and integrated with the rest of his nature. Rather, they were split off from other parts of his personality. They continued to surge into his conscious life, driving him to very ambitious career goals for which he had an incomplete foundation.

His early selfobject relationships reflected his seeking women whom he saw as vitally alive and creative but rootless and lost. He would provide a home and be the sustaining selfobject that would enable the woman to grow. Through her growth he would then be able to ride her coattails and grow as well. This early setting, from which he developed low expectations of himself, led him to the distorted thought that people wouldn't respond to his ideas and talents. Therefore, he needed to develop an upscale network of people and connections who would get things for him rather than his earning them directly.

The impact of the loss of his relationship to Selena was understood in this enlarged context and offered interpretively to him. We were dealing not only with loss of a loved object but the threatened breakup and enfeeblement of his core. Through Selena and her family's connections, Philippe enjoyed greater self-esteem and almost limitless business opportunities. With both of their talents and his business sense, they did develop a successful nascent business. However, the business needed her family's money to capitalize its growth. She left him just at that pivotal time for her father's choice of husband, so the business and his dreams of success were destroyed.

These hypotheses about his relationships, blocks to success, and difficulties in affect regulation formed the basis for the focal problems to be
addressed in his therapy. We talked about the need to help him mourn the
relationship with Selena. We talked of the importance of understanding
his need to pick certain women with whom to form repetitive, archaic
selfobject relationships that were probably doomed because of their primi-
tive, self-focused nature. We talked of the need to improve ways of regulating his feelings along with correcting his distorted self image. I also
wanted to further assess the nature and extent of his self-diagnosed dyslexia. He agreed with the goals for his therapy.

We then discussed the length of time he was able and willing to com-
mit. He felt comfortable with the idea of coming for about three months.
I suggested that we would prioritize what could be done in this time frame.
This meant focusing on the mourning, outlining the repetitive girlfriend
pattern, helping him to identify his selfobject needs, and addressing what
would happen internally and behaviorally when he was thwarted. We would
reevaluate as we went along.

The Beginning Phase of Treatment of Rosalie

Rosalie, an extremely neat, attractive 18-year-old of West Indian descent,
presented in a coy, quiet, polite manner and looked younger than her age.
This contrasted to the psychologically sophisticated way in which she
expressed herself when she chose to speak. She scanned the office and
offered that it was nice. When I asked how she felt being here she indicated solemnly that it was "a very big step to take." She had made the decision herself to seek treatment. I mirrored back what an important and
positive step that was for her and asked if she would explain what was troubling her.

She whispered in a somewhat conspiratorial tone that since graduating
from high school last spring she had remained at home and neither worked
nor went to college. She easily described being depressed in the sense that
she slept a lot, felt sad a lot, was losing weight, and was unable to mobilize
herself. She felt she was probably disappointing her parents as well.

Unsure of the depth of her depression I delicately probed about possible urges to use self-punishing behaviors and about suicidal/homicidal
ideation. She icily answered no to each. I observed to her that my questions seemed to bother her, and I asked, "How come? " She declared, "Just
because I don't want to kill myself doesn't mean I don't have problems." I

empathically agreed and then asked if she felt others around her also were not understanding how much she was struggling now. She replied that her family and friends weren't very sympathetic, even though her mother endorsed her coming to a therapist. I tried to mirror her state and added that it must be a very confusing and lonely time for her. She relaxed a little more then.

Rosalie enjoyed occasionally socializing with a few friends but they were unavailable most of the day and she never went out at night. She was unable to explain what started this retreat from life but it began in her last year at school. For most of her school life she excelled, until the spring of her senior year. She found it very difficult academically and was traumatized by the idea that she might fail and not graduate. Now she felt if she tried to go to college or work (although she had worked part time successfully a year earlier) she would fail there as well. That was so unbearable a thought that she couldn't even try. As the session came to a close, I sensed how painful it was to reveal these fears and asked how this was feeling for her. She replied that she felt better talking about her problems and having what she said accepted, even though it might not make much sense.

We made another appointment, yet she was reluctant to leave. I asked if it might make more sense to meet two times a week for a short period of time, at least to help break down the isolation. She was pleased by this and indicated that this was the first time all week she had gotten dressed during the day. I was still concerned about not being clear about the extent of her depression and dysfunction in general. Yet I didn't want to exaggerate the degree of her difficulties so I simply reminded her of my availability 24 hours a day via voice mail.

I had the glimmer of two possible focal issues. The first was that she was so narcissistically invested in herself that such an inability to perform at her usual high standards was terrifying to her and a terrible blow to her self-esteem and sense of mastery. The other possibility was that she was having trouble going to the next developmental stage. Staying at home might be a way to avoid issues around separation/individuation. This led to the need to explore her relationship with her family. In what ways was the self–selfobject matrix in which she lived at home providing what she needed to help her grow, and in what ways was it making growth difficult for her?

The next session, a few days later, focused on how her family environment affected her focal problems and to what extent it could be considered a set of resources. It seemed that her parents, especially her mother, were having problems in allowing her to become more autonomous. While her parents were overprotective, they both worked full time; the family spent little time together except on weekends. However, the parents provided some psychological and other material resources to her.

Rosalie was the oldest of three children. While her middle brother was having power struggles with the parents as well, he took the path of becoming as scarce and independent of his family as possible. The younger brother was in Rosalie's charge much too often for her. She spent a lot of time bitterly ventilating how unfair and differently they treated her in contrast to her brothers. Just voicing these feelings toward her family enabled her to feel better than she had in a while, she indicated.

I inquired about other social supports and possible selfobjects. She felt close to her father's sister and her cousin. She felt more able to talk about her interest in boys with her aunt. But she was afraid that if she visited there too much her aunt and her mother would feel she was overstaying her welcome. She has a few girlfriends to whom she revealed little of emotional importance.

At the end of the session, partly to assess the level of her psychological mindedness, I asked if she thought there was a connection between her difficulties with her parents' behavior and her difficulties in school and her withdrawal at home. She agreed that they happened at the same time. She felt somehow that her struggle in school and withdrawal were connected in that she was very afraid to try anything and to fail. But she didn't understand how problems with her parents were connected to her fear of failure and withdrawal. She was now a little curious about herself.

Rosalie's desire for short-term therapy was internally determined. I felt that while she was somewhat depressed, her underlying focal issue around stalled self growth dictated that I encourage her to be her own center of initiative by following her lead in the rest of her therapy. I felt it would be more useful to leave the therapy somewhat more unstructured than with other clients both in terms of length of treatment and design of each session. We will come back to Rosalie later.

MIDDLE AND END PHASES OF THERAPY

The middle and end phases of therapy are condensed into one in brief therapy. There should be a working alliance between the client and therapist. During this phase selfobject transference to the therapist may intensify both positively and negatively; it surges and then recedes. Transferential reactions need to be explored but probably won't be fully resolved. The client will have learned to identify and begin to accept his selfobject needs. Self-state changes in response to his needs getting met or thwarted will be outlined. The self-preserving defenses, distorted expectations, and maladaptive interpersonal patterns will be further identified. Optimally, the client will have begun to identify and to develop more selfobject resources and support in the environment.

Like the beginning, the emphasis is on taking the work in sessions out and applying it to the client's daily life. This means (1) directing more of the transference interpretations to the client's other important self–selfobject relationships, and (2) encouraging changing attitudes, feelings, and behaviors so as to fortify the client's self, especially around the focal issue. Doing so keeps the goals of treatment and termination always present. This also diffuses the focus on the therapy transference and provides a buffer from therapy-induced regression. Cognitive-behavioral techniques may be offered to the client. They aid in the work on the focal issues and form part of the selfobject functions that the therapist provides.

The pace of the beginning of brief therapy may feel similar to that of longer-term therapy, but the pace of the subsequent phase does not. The therapist needs to engage the client deeply and then, as the relationship is established, to make plans for those developmentally appropriate selfobject functions to be dealt with elsewhere in the client's self–selfobject world. The therapist needs to be aware of countertransference manifestations here in terms of the need for completion.

Progress on the focal goals, which is continuously monitored, is identified by the middle phase. If it seems to the patient and the therapist that the goals won't be attained by the end of the contract, that becomes the session topic. Were the focal goals too ambitiously defined? Should the goals be renegotiated or the time limit extended? Are there patient or therapist issues around termination that would affect the decision to extend treatment? What coverage does the managed care company provide? Further exploration is required here. Often peer supervision or formal supervision is helpful to the therapist in this thorny area.

In brief self psychological therapy the therapist needs to keep in mind that the therapy relationship is paramount for the therapy to be effective. The timing of incorporating specific techniques or interventions needs to be considered in their impact on this relationship. Invariably, in the workshops I have conducted therapists ask how does my use of specific techniques and making my approach explicit affect the transference. Some worry that these interventions will be perceived as de-idealizing and will undermine treatment. While this is possible, those therapists who have used this approach usually find the opposite, that is, there may be a tendency for the therapist to be viewed as a magician on whom one may become dependent. This tendency is addressed in two ways: through exploration of the transference, and by making the approach explicit, which then empowers the client to help himself.

Hilary: The Middle Phase

Hilary, a 24-year-old single woman, worked long hours in the advertising field. She was the oldest of five siblings of an economically successful family. She reluctantly sought assistance because she was having episodic bouts of depression and was unable to get over her upset about her roommate's insensitivity to her. She couldn't identify what caused her depression. All that Hilary was aware of regarding her roommate problem was that she had seen her roommate through several big emotional crises, but when Hilary had her own serious difficulties her roommate would dismiss her concerns.

Hilary had seen other therapists over the years when she was negotiating some separation from her family. She experienced her first therapist as a very supportive one who helped her to see that her low self-esteem had to do with how she and her family interacted. She had tried therapy again as an adult after being raped by someone she dated. The trauma had pounded both her self-esteem and trust in other people. Unfortunately, she found these therapists to be either very unresponsive or judgmental of her sexual behavior.

By the time Hilary came to me she was wary. The first few sessions were spent developing a working relationship and helping her to identify the triggers of her depression. Her unspoken expectations that I would be insensitive and dismissive of her troubles were explored and linked up to her low expectations of other important people in her life. My efforts at understanding her wariness and validating those feelings and expectations as reasonable facilitated working together. Hilary seemed to be protecting her self from states of deflation and emptiness induced by another therapy failure by not hoping for too much from me.

Hilary had spent half of the fourth session discussing how puzzled she was over her roommate's behavior. I had learned that her obsession with her roommate signaled a theme of her feeling hurt and angry over a lack of resonance to her feeling state. She then later shifted to going home for the holidays. She felt she was the family slave and was always expected to be at every function and provide for others. She experienced her parents as uncaring and lacking emotional interest in her. In contrast, she perceived her younger brother as a star in the family for being male. The addictive behavior of her younger sister was denied as they all admired her beauty and outgoing personality.

Despite knowing all this, Hilary very much wanted to feel connected to a family during the holidays. But she was very worried about feeling neglected and deflated by the end, which always incapacitated her for a few days thereafter. Her therapist suggested that her difficulty accepting her roommate's insensitivity probably was connected to the neglect she had so often experienced within her family. Given the lack of attunement from her family and roommate, she had no place for the hurt and anger she experienced. She seemed pleased to have sense made of her perceived "overreactions."

She looked wistfully at me as she reiterated how she wished she could prevent this scenario from happening if she went home. I asked if she was wishing that I could provide her with something to protect herself from this anticipated disturbance. She sheepishly agreed that she did, although she knew it was unrealistic. I thought it was important to validate her wishes and to identify the possible reasons why she might become upset in this family experience. I mirrored how frustrating and lonely it was to be with her family and get that kind of nonresponse from them. Hilary seemed pleased that I understood what she experienced, but what could she do about it?

I said that, unfortunately, we were not going to be able to resolve her issues with her family in the next ten minutes. But we could try to figure out what Hilary could do in that situation to at least minimize her feeling of being taken advantage of, and how she could address her own wishes so as reduce her deflated response upon her return to her apartment. I also suggested that Hilary take a small step forward and remain true to her sense of reality by not going along with one of the little denial behaviors she would experience with her family. With agreement on the goals for her home visit, we figured out together concretely what those steps might be.

Hilary came up with some ways of enjoying the time at home with other friends and relatives and with solitary activities as well. We identified positive affective experiences with cousins she could invoke to maintain her

self-esteem and positive image of herself. This would help flood out the
negative and debilitating thoughts she would internalize from holidays with
her family. We also came up with her employing body exercise and yoga
to ground herself and relax.

Her holidays were successfully negotiated. Hilary continued to spend
time with her family but in more selective ways and with reduced frequency.
She became more assertive in her family and with her friends about her
own needs, which she felt alleviated her depression. She stopped after two
more sessions to assess her need for further help and resumed three months
later for six more sessions to work on her relationships with men.

Rachel: The Middle Phase

Rachel, a schoolteacher, came from a southern family that believed in the
bootstrap philosophy of mental health. She thought she should solve all
her own problems and was suspicious of what therapy could do for her.
But she was falling deeper into an immobilizing pit of numbing depression
and couldn't figure out why. With several failed relationships and a new
divorce decree under her belt, she was terrified that she was now in love. It
didn't help that the tick of her biological clock was now a roar in her ears.
Yet, she didn't want another marital disaster. She wondered if there was a
dysfunctional pattern in her relationships with men.

The beginning phase of treatment was a particularly delicate time despite her psychological mindedness because of her wariness about therapy.
As part of the effort to establish rapport with this client, which included
beginning to provide some selfobject functions, I mirrored her concerns
about treatment. I also offered interpretations about the double blow of
narcissistic injury and family disloyalty she may have felt in her decision
to come into therapy.

Her thoughts and feelings were generally split from each other. I piqued
her curiosity about why she might be experiencing symptoms of depression and offered explanations that would help her integrate her thoughts
and behavior with newly identified affect states. I sensed a therapeutic
alliance growing. She was giving greater validity to her needs and feelings,
and was tentatively reaching out to me as an idealized selfobject who would
help her articulate and validate her inner experience without unilaterally
defining her experience for her.

Although Rachel's main issue was depression, as experienced in her
relationships, I refrained from focusing on the therapy transference as long

as negative elements were not manifested. Given the limited time, it seemed more useful to focus on her transferential relationship to other significant people in her self–selfobject environment.

Work got under way about her fears and negativity about her selfobject needs—to be admired, mirrored, and to be in a twinship—and her contempt for those same needs in her partners. We looked at her ambivalence about closeness and the pattern of her relationships. She wondered, would she mess up this current relationship even though her choice of a man was much better this time? She was unconsciously about to test it.

An incident happened at work that Rachel wanted to share with her new lover and partner, a school principal. She described how in a group of people only she stood up to her boss, her own principal, about a serious breach of ethics on the part of the vice principal. However, she was disappointed with herself for not being as articulate as she usually was and for not being able to sway the principal to her side.

I interrupted the flow of her narrative, knowing that her desire to share with her new partner was also a significant test of his attunement to her. To check out my hypothesis I asked how she was feeling about herself regarding this incident. She seemed surprised to become aware of any feelings about it and admitted after a few moments that she was feeling kind of vulnerable. I suggested that we look at this in more detail than usual because it may reflect an important wish and expectation that she has of people to whom she is close. Internally, I felt she was heading toward an experience of selfobject misattunement with her partner that would reaffirm the fact that she shouldn't get close to anyone.

We agreed that her partner's response was going to be important. I asked what she hoped would happen in sharing with him. Surprised at the question, she admitted, also with some surprise, that she wanted some validating support from him. I then asked what kind of response she expected. She realized where we were heading and added that since he was a principal himself, he might miss her psychological needs and respond by explaining school politics to her or, worse, by siding with her principal. She anticipated that she would react angrily to him and feel hopeless inside for letting herself get close to someone. He would be confused and angry and withdraw and feel less hopeful about this budding relationship as well. "Wow," she said. "If that's so, how can I head that off?" I indicated that I was focusing on this incident as a model of how to gain responsiveness from others as well as to help her set the current situation back on an attuned course.

In the next few sessions we identified the strategy of going back to therapy basics when she was unsure of herself. For her that meant getting in touch with her feelings, thoughts, and expectations, and her anticipated response. In terms of the current situation that meant she would have to convey part of her wish to her partner at a time and place that would maximize his responding to her.

She had learned to better identify and value her inner thoughts and feelings instead of experiencing them as liabilities. Soon after she acknowledged this, we both talked of how she could carry on what she learned outside therapy and after therapy ended.

ENDING EMPATHIC BRIEF TREATMENT

Termination is begun when the therapist and client agree that the focal goals are being met. Ideally, the goals will have been accurately estimated within the time frame allotted. Goal attainment entails the client's (1) understanding the self psychological issues underlying the presenting problems that put him at risk, and reducing his self vulnerability around the focal issue; (2) identifying and starting to modify the specific maladaptive affective and cognitive intrapsychic patterns (defenses, distorted expectancies, signs of fragmentation and deflation, roots of rage, and shame reactions) and behaviors that felt so burdensome; and (3) reaching out to others to enhance his sustaining self–selfobject environment. As the focal goals are reached, the therapist should positively acknowledge the event with the client and mirror the client's satisfaction in his efforts.

The selfobject transference to the therapist may have taken on several aspects by the time therapy is ended. Often the relationship is left in a somewhat idealized state. However, since emphases have been placed on reaching out to other selfobject relationships from the beginning of therapy, the traditional dependency appears less of an issue in brief self psychological treatment.

Nonspecific goals include the client's experiencing his self as more cohesive, enlivened, and organized as a result of the therapist's empathic understanding and attunement. Consequently he feels more entitled to pursue his developmentally appropriate needs, is more resilient in the face of frustrations, and can better use his problem-solving skills to attain his goals. The client now has some tools to continue self maintenance and possibly to grow.

Setting the Date for Termination

Whenever possible, use the patient's subjective calendar for determining the actual date. Discuss with the client what a natural cycle of beginning and end of treatment would be for him. It may prove more helpful for some clients to have the treatment phased out by spreading out the last two to three sessions to give him a chance to put into action what was learned and then come back and fine-tune the skills. For some it may be appropriate to space out the last few sessions with increasing time between them.

The therapist needs to give a consistent and firm position on ending the brief treatment. Suggest to clients that minor relapses might occur but to wait a few months to see if they can ultimately address the problem with their new self understanding and resources. Help the clients identify areas of future vulnerability and strategies to prevent or ameliorate them. If the clients can't resolve the new issue or have a serious crisis, consider setting up a new contract to work on the new goal or refer to longer-term treatment when possible.

Clients may face new developmental challenges or have new isolated crises as time goes on. In that case they should be made aware of the possibility of coming in for tune-up sessions in the future to address these issues. Once more the idea of a psychoanalytic "cure" is exchanged for the notion of providing brief, focal therapy throughout life.

Negative Reactions to Termination

Bauer and Kobos (1987) identify and discuss several manifestations of clients' negative reactions to terminating. Some of these reactions are also found in brief self psychological therapy, but are understood and responded to differently. Negative client reactions to ending may include anxiety and anger at terminating, a return of old symptoms, the appearance of new symptoms, devaluation of treatment or the therapist, bargaining for more time to explore further, or a desire to end the therapy early.

Classical and ego psychological approaches would suggest that these reactions are resistances to working through termination, possibly reflecting unresolved conflicts around separation, which may then lead to power struggles. These approaches address these reactions as resistances to completing the work and should be vigorously interpreted. In some dynamic approaches to brief treatment the ending would be the major focus of the treatment itself.

In a self psychological approach, we tend to view these negative responses during termination as resulting from expectable sadness and anxiety over ending and losing the therapist as a valued selfobject. These are legitimate client concerns about how well the client will weather threats to the integrity of his self and if he will lose gains made in brief treatment. Transference interpretations are offered, linking the client's reactions to perceived separations and loss from early selfobjects to the therapist, and to their impact on fears of separation, loss, and abandonment from other current selfobjects. We also celebrate the joy of mastery and work done on the focal goals even during sessions focused on negative reactions.

Potential Countertransference Reactions

Short-term psychotherapy may heighten reactions for the therapist as well as the client both in terms of its brevity and the impact of external reviewers of the service. Bauer and Kobos (1987) report that therapists may become aware during their client's treatment of the reemergence within themselves of issues around dependency, separation, unresolved perfectionism and grandiosity, and guilt over leaving issues unexplored and/or unresolved. This may lead to the therapist's feeling ineffectual, thus devaluing herself as therapist and devaluing the treatment approach.

In providing self psychological therapy the therapist may experience the intensity during treatment as even greater than within other therapy approaches. The therapist is ultimately confronted with the loss of the client as a possible selfobject relationship and the loss of the therapy experience as a selfobject experience that may have provided mastery, growth, and professional stability.

As a result of these countertransferential reactions the therapist needs to be aware of any tendency to dwell too early or too long on termination and not enough on the focal issue, or to deny the importance of termination.

The next chapter discusses in more detail these reactions from the therapist's and client's perspectives.

Samantha: End Phase

In the third to last session Samantha indicated that she was all right with ending. She just wanted to know the door was open if she wanted to resume in the future. I smiled and agreed that of course it was. She went on to say "Part of me is afraid to stop. I don't want to feel that horrible way again and I won't take medication. I'm also afraid that you'll be disappointed with me for leaving." First I pursued where she felt she would be most vulnerable to that anxious mood and obsessional thinking. I then spent the rest of the session exploring her fear of my disappointment, articulating for us how she experienced my help, and how she might experience my needing her to stay as she felt her mother did. The theme here was separation anxiety and fear of abandonment.

We began the next to last session by expressing satisfaction at the work accomplished and sadness over ending. We then reviewed the reasons for coming; her unrelenting work anxiety; the work we had done on it in terms of using empathy to understand her underlying dynamics, needs, and defenses; the self-image she would construct of herself; and consequent behaviors. I also made reference to those genetic aspects of her early selfobject relations that left her with chronic anxiety.

We had seen an impact of the same focal issue on other aspects of her life, such as her intimate relationship. Samantha agreed that her difficulty with anxiety had impact on more areas of her life than she had realized, since it was a seamless part of her. We began to see her anxiety at work as related to perfectionism and the fear that if she is too expansive and assertive she will lose her internal tie to her parents, who might punish her and wither away themselves.

In the last session I further suggested that she try to use a similar approach to identifying and addressing her anxiety in other areas as she did with work issues, that is, to use it as a model for herself. This session I pressed further. I was trying to change her work self concept. I indicated that she now had a few years of work experience under her belt. Work evaluations at her past job were very good. She had passed the probationary period at her current job with flying colors. She was skilled and knew this cognitively. She needed to continue to take small steps to act on her new understanding and view of herself. She suggested we work on her chronic need to have all her graphic presentations looked at by another colleague before sending them off to the client. I was aware of some possible parallel of this topic to her concerns about my reactions to ending therapy. This allowed us to talk about our ending a little more. Then we ended.

In a follow-up session, in terms of her anxieties about her presentations, she felt that they would still be there but to a lesser degree now that she had seen senior staff also flounder in them. She wanted to be more of a senior presence at work and take on more decision making and responsibility, but on her terms. She decided to be proactive and to approach the senior staff about carving out new challenges for her at work that would give her greater visibility and respect while accepting her presentation skills. I commented on how far she had come in engaging in all these psychological steps—reductions in anxiety and immobilizing obsessiveness, a greater sense of entitlement to become visible, and changing things on her own behalf. She asked how I was doing. Once more we looked at the transferential aspect of her reaction where she saw me partly as her frail, loving parent and a disapproving parental imago. But I added that I was fine and was really pleased that she felt better. Perhaps we would talk in the future.

Rosalie: Middle and End Phase

Rosalie was seen twice a week for two weeks. During this time she articulated both her need to be attached to her family and her desire to be more independent of them. Her anger and fears regarding her parents were accessed with greater ease. We began to understand her emotions and behaviors as reactions to her parents' lack of fine attunement to the tendrils of her newly growing self. She admitted that having their support to go out into the world meant she would undertake a scary trip where she might fail. But not having precise attunement from them and getting mixed messages about their support enraged her. This made her feel guilty and bad about herself as well.

As with many teenagers, open disclosure to an adult of feelings and events takes time and trust. We were fortunate that she could now reveal the precipitating events underlying her focal issue. She began to realize that being homebound was somehow a way to deal with her fear of taking risks and failing both at school and at home. I also silently hypothesized that her failed grandiose expectations at school may have led to anger being turned against herself to punish herself. It fed into lowered self-esteem and a negative self concept, which was potentiated by her isolation.

Rosalie had done above-average work most of her school life until now. Her poor grades in high school math devastated her. She then had a charismatic male math teacher who taught her to do well in and love math. However, he didn't return the next year, and she found out that he had died suddenly. Her grades again plummeted in math and then in other areas. She became more and more miserable and dreaded going to school. She barely passed and graduated. Now she was afraid that in whatever she tried she might experience the same struggles and failure.

We explored further the role this charismatic teacher played, especially the link between his leaving, his death, and her fear of trying. The therapist interpreted in simple language that doing poorly in math shook her confidence in her own intelligence and future career goals. It was a humiliating defeat for her and, she assumed, in the eyes of her parents, who saw her as the smart child. The loss of the math teacher (an idealized selfobject, perhaps eroticized) left her in despair that she could ever succeed. She presumed her parents' love and admiration of her and her own self-esteem were greatly diminished.

In this middle phase of Rosalie's therapy her depression became less intense and she began to socialize more with girlfriends. At her request sessions were reduced to once a week. She initially seemed to view me as someone who accepted her attitudes, mirrored her thoughts and feelings, and helped her to integrate them. She felt "it was cool" to talk to this adult, in contrast to her parents. She now also seemed to experience me as someone who could filter, give form to, and help contain her strong emotions. This contributed to her finally revealing how she was struggling with a potential boyfriend.

We then returned to her family conflicts and their contribution to her current withdrawal. She disclosed that the previous summer, right after graduation, she and her mother went to California to visit relatives. Rosalie wanted to stay three days longer with her aunt. Over her mother's objections she changed her plane ticket and stayed.

When she returned home her mother grounded her for the year so that Rosalie couldn't go back to her part-time job, which she enjoyed, nor could she socialize without permission. She could only take college courses. Rosalie became furious at her perceived imprisonment. As time wore on and her mother gave her more freedom, Rosalie decided to demonstrate her autonomy by refusing to go out. Later she became aware that she just became more depressed and didn't even want to go out. In this state several months later she contacted me.

I spent some time helping her to see possible connections between her parental struggles and her symptoms, based on the things she had said earlier. Paraphrasing her, I suggested that from her point of view she was trying to have a little more freedom from family and felt she was being punished for it. However, she was confused and felt guilty for feeling aggressive toward her parents, who had given her so much. And she felt ashamed of her poor grades in her parents' eyes. She feared being further emotionally ignored and abandoned by them. In her desperate effort to become more independent, she was imprisoning herself further at home. This imprisonment was no victory at all, and her parents still seemed to be unaware that she was growing up. Worse, it eroded her confidence about being in the world.

She perceived that there was no one to mirror her efforts and accomplishments and no one to consistently encourage her self to expand, take risks, and begin to explore her ambitions and goals. Neither her anxious mother nor her workaholic father could help soothe her when she didn't perform at her usually high standards. She felt she couldn't turn to her younger aunts for help in integrating her budding sexual interests because her mother would experience it as disloyalty. The one adult who had faith in her and helped her to feel confident left her and died without any notice. All this deflated her self-esteem and made her despair of her wishes and struggles to be understood. She was experiencing her self as less vital and increasingly prone to psychological injury. Withdrawal was simultaneously punitive and self-protective.

In the next few sessions Rosalie described feeling less depressed, more sociable, and more confident. She had identified that ultimately she wanted to become a chiropractor. But now she'd like to get a full-time job rather than be pushed into college by her parents.

We now worked on her struggles with her boyfriend. She rarely saw him due to his work hours and her mother's limit setting. She revealed her disillusionment with her boyfriend and with men in general about demanding sex whenever they were together. She said that he had ended their relationship over her "holding back on sex." She was angry and hurt, had gotten depressed and then drunk over the weekend while her family was away. I tried to explore nonjudgmentally what she was feeling and what the alcohol did for her. She described how it numbed her impotent rage and unheard hurt. With some encouragement she confronted her boyfriend over the phone and felt stronger and freer as a result.

Rosalie canceled before the next session because she was going to a job interview. She was excited about earning her own money and getting out of the house but was scared about being accepted. Whether or not she could articulate her intrapsychic changes, she seemed less depressed and able to be more in the world, all this despite her boyfriend having ended their relationship. She was getting ready to separate from her current selfobject relationship.

In the last two sessions Rosalie reported feeling less depressed and less withdrawn. Some days she had to push herself to go out, but she always felt better when she did. She felt angry and somewhat deceived about her boyfriend, but was no longer grieving. Her parents were restoring more of her freedoms. The focus of these sessions was on her excitement and fear about working and her reactions to her family's pleasure at her working.

She talked of taking a vacation with her friends with the money she would earn on her new job. Her idea was to reveal the plan to her parents when it was all in place to prove to them that she could be responsible enough to go. While it seemed that she was testing her parents' limits it was a more mature version than her earlier trip.

I brought up her missing or coming late to sessions recently. Internally I wondered if it signaled progress or regression and rebellion. We then talked about her now erratic attendance and future appointments. She voiced that maybe she was feeling ready to end therapy. Rosalie was pleased about her progress but scared about ending. She was not as needful about coming but requested my support during her transition to working part time. She wanted to discontinue scheduled sessions for now and call for an appointment if she needed my assistance. Given her age and the nature of her issues I agreed to her plan.

We decided to look at upcoming situations that might give her trouble. She indicated that she was fearful of not performing well at her new job in the eyes of her superiors. She also feared being an outsider among her work peers. I mirrored back how frightening the unknown can be and then suggested that what she was anticipating sounded like it was based on other experiences of hers. She admitted that taking this job felt like starting high school—very scary and competitive. She was concerned about being judged by her bosses and by her peers. We talked about the different expectations of a job versus school and what kinds of difficult situations she anticipated. Then we focused on what options she could provide to herself. I reminded her that what frightened her and most people was the feeling of being trapped and helpless and that we could now identify some work strategies.

At the end she recalled that the day she started kindergarten she was very excited, didn't cry, and just told her mother that she could go home now! Rosalie was pleased with her restored confidence and the fledgling steps she was taking. She was indeed working on her issues of separation and growth and could now retrieve a positive memory of such experiences with which to assist her in her next developmental stage.

CHAPTER 6

THERAPIST AND CLIENT ISSUES WITH BRIEF THERAPY

The chapters on conducting short-term therapy with individuals and couples are meant to encourage both novice and experienced therapists in their efforts to do systematic, empathic, brief work. To maximize that experience and to minimize the instabilities caused by the brief and probably managed treatment, it is useful to identify potential problems in brief work. Keep in mind that the health care climate continues to evolve and seems to be more sensitive now to the impact of managed care on the quality of the health service provided.

The focus here is on the range of reactions that a therapist and client may have to each other as a result of their interactions in brief therapy. It goes beyond transferential and countertransferential dynamics and includes the impact of the managed care organization on the self–selfobject dyad.

GENERAL PROBLEMATIC REACTIONS TO THE BRIEF THERAPY EXPERIENCE

Hoyt and Farrell (1984) suggest that the act of accepting a client into treatment and its attendant unconscious obligation may already predispose the therapist to countertransferential reactions. They quote Racker (1968): "What motive (in terms of the unconscious) would the analyst have for wanting to cure if it were not he who made the patient ill? In this way the patient is already, simply by being a patient, the creditor, the accuser, the 'superego' of the analyst; and the analyst is his debtor" (p. 146). Layered on top of these reactions may be the therapist's reactions to having to play this role within a short-term therapy situation.

The first of these reactions is the therapist's anticipated "resistance" to conducting brief therapy, which needs to be reframed. Good supervision, therapy, and peer support for the clinician help in dealing with such reactions and self states. In conducting therapy with a client, I believe it is more useful and accurate to try to understand and even validate the therapist's difficulty in embracing brief therapy. To say one is resisting also begs the question of what is internally going on for that person around that particular issue.

Clinicians' anticipated resistance to brief treatment reflects a wide range of understandable personal and professional issues. On the personal side, therapists' anticipated economic instability and need to market their practice more often and aggressively, giving up of current professional skills, and learning whole new approaches are often mentioned as deflating, frightening, enraging, and humiliating prospects. They worry that they will be working much harder for much less income. The greater emotional ups and downs in forming a relationship in brief therapy and then having to terminate so soon are perceived as potentially taking a high toll on therapists.

On the professional side, there is a natural anxiety and anger at having to use a modality one was not trained in. Also, therapists, especially seasoned psychodynamic therapists, are dubious of short-term therapy doing anything more than providing support. If we view the therapist as having a professional "self," then we can see how health care changes threaten to subjectively alter clinicians' professional self-identity and undermine their sense of mastery, vitality, and esteem.

Once they start conducting brief therapy, dynamic therapists feel pressure to intervene or interpret before there is enough information regarding the client. This pressure is especially acute for the empathic therapist, for whom enabling the patient to feel understood is so essential to the treatment. Brief therapy is also perceived to engender feelings of guilt in performing inadequately and separation anxiety in the clinician.

The therapist can become more comfortable with taking interpretive risks if she views the treatment as a collaborative effort, with the client sharing in the work. I also believe that patients are usually forgiving when we are off the mark if we offer our understanding and frame interpretations as hypotheses rather than as certainties. They are also more understanding if we demonstrate that we are trying to be attuned to their selfobject needs and are willing to explore their reactions to any empathic breaches to which we may have contributed.

Novice therapists tend personally to have an easier time learning and applying their short-term therapy skills to clients. But while seasoned dynamic therapists may have difficulty adapting to short-term therapy, it is clear that the more seasoned therapist, who is well rounded in theories, techniques, and experience, may be able to assess better and more quickly, have a more complete set of tools to help a wider array of clients, and may not become as overwhelmed by more difficult clients as their junior colleagues.

Hoyt (1985), a strong advocate for brief therapy, identified several assumptions about long-term and short-term dynamic psychotherapy that may add to therapists' resistance to doing brief work. The first assumption was that longer-term psychotherapy produced more impressive and more lasting resolution of the problems that brought a client into treatment. As previously mentioned, psychotherapy research is simply not conclusive here. Hoyt and many other therapists additionally question the value of any added gains of long-term therapy when weighed against the additional time and money. He advocates for the positive benefit of a time-limited approach, which he believes heightens the client's rapid and active engagement in the treatment process.

Hoyt challenges some of the theoretical assumptions of why treatment must take a long time to be effective. They include the belief that the therapeutic alliance must form slowly, that the patient must be allowed to regress so that pathological early experiences can be uncovered slowly and fully, that the transference requires a length of time to develop and to be interpreted, and that a lengthy working-through process is required for gains to be consolidated. He counters those assumptions about long-term work with opposing assumptions about short-term treatment, albeit with selected clients. They include the belief that with selected clients a working alliance could be formed quite early, that clients could benefit from early interpretation of the transference, that focused treatment could mobilize the whole system to begin changing, that generalized regression in itself is not useful and should be confined to the focal area, that repeated interpretations of the triangle of transference facilitate the consolidation of gains throughout treatment, and that reactions to termination could be interpreted throughout the short-term treatment with clients who can tolerate separation anxiety.

He adds that, on the other hand, one also needs to be aware of client and therapist resistance to engaging in exploratory psychotherapy as well. Either therapist or client may choose short-term treatment to avoid dealing with upsurges in issues of intimacy and dependency. The therapist or client may opt for brief work as a way to quickly experience some success. Other therapists may find the working-through process, so necessary for some clients' treatment, to be tedious.

I agree with Hoyt that a skilled clinician should first assess what is best for a client, that is, open-ended therapy, longer-term therapy, or time-limited, short-term treatment, when the therapist and client have the ability to choose.

ASPECTS OF MANAGED CARE THAT TRIGGER THERAPIST AND CLIENT REACTIONS

When initially confronted with a managed care environment, therapists may feel traumatized, humiliated, and even impotent. Some may then go into mourning. They may feel that their professional identity has been devalued and may possibly be eliminated. There is anxiety over losing their livelihood. Once they start working within the managed care settings, clinicians have strong doubts about their ability to truly help their clients. At times they may be conflicted about doing what is good for the client in the short run versus the long run. They may experience conflicts between their professional interests and the client's interests. For example, therapists may have to deal with externally imposed limits on the number and length of sessions. If they choose to request more appropriate treatment for their clients, they may fear generating a poor profile with the managed care provider.

They may also find that acceptable treatment modalities are somewhat restrictive. Consequently, therapists have to learn new approaches to treatment, and, often, a new set of professional values. In addition to having patients as clients, therapists have to learn to negotiate with a third party who may not be psychologically sophisticated.

Issues of confidentiality are one manifestation of increased concerns about therapists' liability. Other liability issues may include therapists' responsibility for perceived incomplete or inappropriate care.

Clearly the structure of the psychotherapy experience and the therapy relationship is altered when a third party is involved. How much the client will respond to the involvement of the managed care organization and the kind of client response partly depend on our understanding of what managed care means for us as therapists and what attitudes we convey about this third party to the client.

Saakvitne and Abrahamson (1994) cogently discuss the impact of doing longer-term psychoanalytic therapy under managed care, which has some relevance to doing dynamic brief therapy as well. In terms of change in the structure or frame of the treatment, they point to the managed care organization's impact on fees and payment, boundaries around confidentiality, and "autonomy of practice" (p. 186).

Under managed care, what the client pays and how and when the therapist collects his fee are altered. The client pays a small part of the fee and the managed care organization pays the rest upon submission of a valid claim. As a result, therapeutic interpretations about payment behavior will also need to be modified.

Money in psychotherapy can tend to become a hidden, neglected issue in general. The more the therapist prepares himself for doing this kind of work and the more he understands what money issues mean for him, given his background, the easier will be his transition to dealing with money in this setting.

With each client the therapist will need to understand what co-paying for treatment means for the client and what it means when he doesn't make the co-payment. If plans are made to continue with the therapist beyond the coverage allotted, then they will both have to discuss from the outset how it will affect the treatment if the money arrangement changes.

While the therapy becomes more complex when someone other than the client pays for it, it does have its positive side for some kinds of clients. For those who fear relying on a therapist because they will be wanted for their money, having a third party pay may relieve them of that fear and allow them to form a therapeutic alliance.

Confidentiality is altered by insurance review and concurrent case management. Like the money issue, much of the impact of the managed care organization can be contained if the therapist prepares herself for doing managed care work. This preparation precedes her explaining the parameters of therapy to each client in the first session. Limits of confidentiality and required episodic authorization especially need to be spelled out.

Third-party involvement in case review would be more acceptable to clinicians if they knew that the reviewers were properly trained (trained psychologically and bound by confidentiality restraints as well) and sensitive to the impact of review on the therapy relationship. On the other hand, it may be beneficial for clinicians to share their clinical thought processes and therapy work with others regularly.

Clients are understandably anxious about receiving appropriate, adequate, and affordable treatment. Their concern is especially heightened when the modality of brief treatment is externally determined. New brief therapists, in turn, describe how this adds pressure to their allaying clients' anxieties when they aren't yet fully aware of and confident in helping the clients. Clients' anxiety about the therapist's ability to help may also be experienced by the therapist as a blow to her professional self-esteem.

Uncertainties about the continuance of treatment beyond the typical eight to ten sessions may cause a considerable undercurrent of anxiety and stress in both therapist and client. For the client this may take the form of separation anxiety or a deeper anticipatory anxiety about experiencing a state of depletion and fragmentation over the loss of a sustaining selfobject. For more impaired clients this uncertainty may even trigger annihilation anxiety where the client fears the loss of his self. Clearly, provisions need to be made for these clients at the outset to mobilize multiple resources and to improve their entire support system.

Other common potential reactions to the uncertainty of treatment include the client's concern about the limited power and the trustworthiness of the therapist. There can be a narcissistic injury to both therapist and client when a client is allotted only a few sessions of coverage or denied further care beyond the initial approved number of visits. The meaning of this event needs to be understood for both members of the dyad. The temptation may be great for client and therapist to deny and ward off experiencing the therapist as de-idealized (and therefore the client experiencing himself as devalued and defeated) by forging an alliance against the managed care organization. The wish is that by verbally allying against the managed care organization the self–selfobject relationship between patient and therapist is restored as an enlivening and empowering one.

The time-limited aspect of managed care treatment can impact the therapist–client relationship in yet another way. That is, both client and therapist may feel pressure for the client to be "cured" within the allotted time. If the client doesn't seem to be improving the therapist may begin to feel anxious and frustrated with the client for being uncooperative. The therapist's experience of ineffectiveness and failure with resultant feelings of helplessness and shame may also be projected onto the "bad" client as well as the managed care organization. For some therapists the pressure may feel so great that they may develop split-off wishes to abandon the client or the therapeutic process.

When clinicians have to justify further treatment to a managed care organization they become "the hero, the partner in crime, the protective parent, the corrupt schemer who gets the system to work for him, and when it fails the perpetrator, the nonprotective bystander, or the victim" (Saakvitner and Abrahamson 1994, p. 191). This difficult situation needs to be addressed in several ways. The time-limited nature of the treatment needs to be spelled out clearly at the beginning of treatment. The uncertainties of the ultimate length of treatment need to be explored and understood by both client and therapist. Together they need to look at how these factors affect their view of the therapist and feelings about the therapy itself.

For a host of humane, ethical, and legal reasons the therapist and client need to discuss alternative plans should the client need more care beyond his authorized treatment. The therapist may also need to pave the way for the client to be seen by another facility or therapist. In this difficult circumstance the therapist needs to contain his sense of guilt and narcissistic rage so that the client can work through his own reactions and start anew.

In empathic brief psychotherapy the therapist and client need to continuously monitor progress toward the client's goals, which also keeps the treatment's time limit in the foreground. Empathic treatment also continuously focuses the treatment outward toward a more sustaining selfobject and object world rather than on the curative role of the therapist alone. This focus ameliorates some of the impact of the nature of brief treatment under managed care.

Another issue for the client relates to what the managed care organization will and will not cover. Most managed care organizations will approve treatment that addresses symptoms affecting basic daily functioning. Inadvertently, this narrowed criterion for approved care may be experienced by the client as discounting the validity of the need for psychotherapy. The wish to pursue wellness and psychological growth rather than restoration of basic psychological function may be internalized by the client as a quixotic or completely self-indulgent enterprise. The client may then project that the therapist feels the same negative way about those goals.

Client splitting between the good therapist and bad managed care organization (case manager) is another possibility. As always, the function of the splitting needs to be understood as a particular way to preserve the client's self and the process of healing the split must begin. The split may provide a way to preserve the therapist as a powerful, loving selfobject in the face of the managed care organization's perceived intrusion. The split may also be a vehicle with which to displace the client's anger at the therapist onto the managed care organization as a result of some client–therapist interaction.

USE OF ADJUNCTS TO SHORT-TERM PSYCHOTHERAPY

In this chapter we have been outlining some important issues that could potentially disrupt the selves of the client and therapist and the curative selfobject relationship they would create together. Many of these issues relate to the requirement to use brief treatment to treat clients all along the continuum of mental health. Empathic brief psychotherapy provides a way of helping an array of clients with its emphasis on the attuned therapist's initiating or enhancing the client's self–selfobject environment. Toward that end the brief, self psychotherapist may recruit other modalities that will enhance the client's selfobject functioning. For example, combining group therapy with individual therapy is a powerful therapeutic experience where the two modalities have a synergistic therapeutic effect on the client.

Some adjuncts to individual therapy that clinicians have found helpful include bibliotherapy (the use of educative, personal growth books and tapes), self-help groups, hypnotherapy, eye movement desensitization and reprocessing (EMDR), body therapy work, yoga, exercise, and pharmacotherapy. The choice of an adjunct to psychotherapy needs to be tailored to the needs and goals of the particular client. Preferably it should be something that is consistent with what we know of the client. It needs to be introduced in a sensitive way and its meaning for the client explored.

Ben, a 54-year-old free-lance advertising consultant, was chronically anxious, had trouble falling asleep, and was obsessive-compulsive and isolated. After five therapy sessions he had begun to calm down as we identified and started to work on his underlying focal issue related to inadequate self soothing and affect containment. His sleep deprivation was becoming intolerable, yet he refused anything perceived as artificial. I asked if he ever had any hobbies and he replied that years ago he ran. We explored why he stopped and then how would it feel to try it again since it might tire him enough to aid his sleep. We discussed what it would mean for him to make this change in his life and its potential to become compulsive. He agreed to it. He decided to run regularly. Running has helped to give structure to his day, he has met other runners, and he has less trouble falling asleep.

Medication

Therapists have been divided about the use of psychotropic medication concurrently with psychotherapy, especially in psychoanalytically oriented therapy (Beitman 1991). In general, therapists are concerned with the potential of drugs for interfering with the organic, evolving nature of treatment. Whether the therapist prescribes the medication or instead works with a psychopharmacologist is thought to have impact on the therapist, the client, and their working relationship. Here are some of the articulated reasons.

Needing to medicate a client may be experienced as a blow to the professional self-esteem of the therapist for not being able to provide all that is necessary to help the client. Collaborating around medication may feel like a crapshoot. Not knowing the psychopharmacologist well may make a therapist feel anxious about the quality of care the client is receiving. The therapist may also fear exposure of his work with the client, fear that the client will prefer to work with the colleague, or even fear that the client will be stolen away by the colleague. The therapist may also worry about how the managed care organization views the need for the client to be medicated with regard to the competence of the therapist. Concerns over how a client's defenses may be modified by seeing another mental health practitioner arise. For example, certain kinds of clients may engage in splitting, making therapy more difficult.

When the therapist himself does the medicating, the client may come to feel that the therapist is positively omnipotent or menacingly intrusive into his body and mind. Clients taking medication may become deflated and frightened over their perceived failure to help themselves. Taking medication may cause the client to de-idealize the therapist at a crucial, inappropriate time in the treatment where the client needs a containing, soothing, or enlivening selfobject to internalize.

The impact of the medication itself on the body and mind of the client needs to be understood. Paradoxically, the successful action of a drug may make a client feel frightened and even more out of control. The same response may result from the impact of drug side effects. Why bother with medication?

Today there have been major advances in the pharmacological treatment of psychological difficulties. Drugs can be employed to reduce symptoms, prevent relapse, facilitate intrapsychic and interpersonal changes, or reduce cost of treatment. I have found that some medications for some clients can prove quite helpful to the therapeutic process and potentiate the effect of the psychotherapy.

Especially in brief psychotherapy we look for ways to enhance and maximize the effectiveness of the treatment. For example, medication for depressed clients may enable them to mobilize their physical and mental resources to literally come and work in the session. Medication for anxious clients may enable them to turn down the background psychic noise so that they can concentrate on what is actually said in session and then act on what they have learned.

Of course, coordinating the medication care of the client means understanding ahead of time how the particular client might experience and react to the medication experience. The client's medication concerns and possible noncompliance need to be empathically understood and not quickly dismissed with reassurances or veiled threats. In addition, it is important for the therapist to learn about the medication, the benefits and risks of taking it, and alternatives to it. Educating the client about side effects can be helpful, too. For several of the newer antidepressant drugs, such as Prozac or Zoloft, it might be helpful to convey to the client that the medication needs to be taken on a regular basis, and to reassure the client that it is not addictive and that it may take a while to really become effective, during which time the side effects should diminish. Clients also need to feel that the therapist will be concerned and receptive to hearing about untoward reactions to the medications without being judgmental.

CHAPTER 7

EMPATHIC BRIEF PSYCHOTHERAPY WITH COUPLES

In the past thirty years psychotherapy has grown and evolved as a modality to include work with couples and families. The high proportion of breakups of marriages and families has drafted therapists to provide assistance, just as World War II drafted clinicians to treat traumatized soldiers. The request for help has extended to unmarried couples living together, both heterosexual and same-sex, as well as to couples living apart in noncommitted relationships. Couples and family therapy have traditionally been conducted in shorter time frames than individual therapy, but the time frame may have shrunk even further in the new health care environment.

BACKGROUND

There have developed several organized schools of family and marital therapy including cognitive-behavioral approaches, systems approaches, and psychoanalytically oriented approaches. Within the psychodynamic school, early marital therapy often employed Freudian concepts, which assumed that partners functioned on an oedipal level. Therapy might involve the exploration and working through of neurotic patterns of marital interaction where the partners would have to learn to give up their infantile neurotic dependency needs.

Since then psychodynamic clinicians have begun to view psychological functioning in more multilinear, multidimensional ways. As a result,
clients manifesting preoedipal difficulties and those with personality and
character disorders were now deemed appropriate for couples therapy.
More recently, greater validity has been given to the subjective realities of
each partner and to healthy interdependence between members of a couple.

In therapy, across the major approaches, couples are helped to resolve
relationship problems by various methods. These methods typically include
improvement of communication skills, negotiation of stated (i.e., conscious)
wants and needs, identification and acceptance of major differences between the partners, and identification of the roles that each partner may
play in the couple/family system that keep it in equilibrium.

But why are these approaches only partially successful or leave the couple
in a psychological cul-de-sac? I believe that for these couples core psychological issues may have been left unaddressed or not given appropriate
priority in treatment.

From a self psychological point of view, one's partner is one of the most
important objects in the self–selfobject matrix of relationships in which
that person is embedded. The couple's central issue is how well each partner is nourished by the other in terms of selfobject needs.

In conducting couples therapy, Lachkar (1985), Schwartzman (1984),
Solomon (1988, 1989), as well as Ringstrom (1994a) and Trop (1994) with
their intersubjective orientation (an outgrowth of self psychology) concur
that the concept of the selfobject provides the clinician with another way
of understanding a couple's behavior. However, couples therapists differ
as to how limited they believe the self psychological approach is to couples
with serious narcissistic pathology.

I believe that in self psychology we have another way of understanding
an aspect of the dynamics of all couples, since everyone has selfobject needs,
not just those people with narcissistic character or personality disorders.
Selfobject strivings do coexist with oedipal (object) strivings past childhood, and each partner of the couple does continuously serve selfobject
functions for the other's self. Couples' conflicts can be more broadly illuminated and treated if we can go beyond explaining couple pathology using
the structural model of intrapsychic conflicts or systems theory alone and
look at the self–selfobject relationships established in childhood that become partly reestablished in adult couples.

Ideal, "healthy" people need selfobject relationships throughout life,
although the nature of those selfobject needs evolve. Healthy people have

selves that they experience as cohesive, vital, and continuous over time. Each partner experiences his self as being the center of initiative for his own person. The need for mirroring, idealizing, and twinship are also limited in duration and reciprocated by each partner over time.

Most people have a less than optimal sense of self yet can still have a good relationship. Solomon (1988) states, "It is possible for the partners to develop a mutual interplay and reciprocity with each other that, while imperfect and subject to the usual stress of living together, may still provide for both a way to be good selfobjects for one another, legitimizing their own archaic needs by developing methods of caring for each other" (p. 219).

COUPLE BREAKDOWN

In applying self psychology to couples therapy Schwartzman (1984) worked with couples who had a variety of diagnostic profiles and varied degrees of self and object differentiation. She concluded that, regardless of their pathologies and personality types, "The extent to which a marital partner failed as a selfobject for the other affected the fate of the marriage" (p. 14).

Certainly a couple's relationship may start to break down for a variety of reasons, such as socioeconomic, physical, and psychological stressors. In the psychological arena, what starts couple breakdown and causes the relationship to fail? I believe it happens as result of chronic dissatisfaction in the self–selfobject experiences with each other. When one's selfobject needs are chronically not acknowledged or responded to, especially by one's partner, then that person is likely to begin to experience internal states of deflation, depletion, and possible fragmentation. That person may be prone to negative self states by anticipating the partner's lack of response, which mirrors being disappointed by early caregivers. The extent and duration of these negative experiences depends on how psychologically vulnerable the person is in general. The person will react to these impending states and take measures to shore up his self by using adaptive measures or maladaptive, regressive ones.

The defenses employed and resultant behavior then have impact on the mate. Responses to lack of attunement may include anger, fear, suspiciousness, shame, withdrawal, extra-couple affairs, and substance abuse. If these responses occur based on a fixed expectation of anticipated disappointment alone rather than actual misattunement, then the mate will be particularly puzzled and upset by the partner's behavior. If the mate is unable or unwilling to see the partner's distress signals, this may increase the pull for the partner to reenact earlier selfobject interchanges with the mate. In this threatened state the partner may need to experience the mate as a part of her own self in order to repair her enfeebled part. Reactions and counterreactions by the partners to these reenactments become magnified unless something can break the cycle of misattunement or a truce is declared so as to keep the couple system in equilibrium.

There is an additional sad irony to this situation. Often people tend to choose partners who experienced similar early selfobject failures but who developed complementary or even opposing patterns of defense to deal with the sequelae of those failures (Gurman 1978, Ringstrom 1994a, Solomon 1988). Often these people defend against reexperiencing any part of those early failures. They are unable to see their common background and how it affected their development, and therefore are unable to help each other with the same need for attunement. As a result, the same individual defensive pattern that is giving the individual trouble is unconsciously reinforced by the couple's dynamics.

> Paul and Sarah* came from unattuned parents who were still struggling to function on their own psychologically. Both partners gave up much hope of their parents' responding to their self needs. Instead they found others outside the family to idealize and they developed healthier selves in those relationships. Sarah needed Paul to be strong and steady but that stance was, for him, partly a result of his sequestering his need for closeness and fear of vulnerability. When she was unable to perceive his disguised need for soothing when stressed, he would become intellectualized, critical, and distant. Because of Paul's need to idealize Sarah, she was unwilling to reveal how often she needed him to soothe and contain her in moments of anxiety and depression, lest she experience her needs as shameful imperfections. In that state of heightened need she was more likely to go into a depression, waiting for him to notice. Rather than each being able to identify and respond to each other's frustration and pain, they each retreated to their own lonely psychological space.

---

*Portions of this case were excerpted from a case presented in a workshop for the Association for Psychoanalytic Self Psychology with J. Magdoff, April 24, 1993. Details have been modified to protect the identity of the clients.

CURRENT MODEL OF APPLYING SELF PSYCHOLOGY TO BRIEF COUPLES TREATMENT

The literature on couples therapy is fairly extensive. Although it is tradi-tionally shorter term than individual therapy, the reader is referred to Budman and Gurman (1988) for material on formally conducting *brief* couples therapy. This chapter focuses on my model of brief self psycho-logically oriented psychotherapy as it applies to couples work. It assumes the reader has some familiarity with conducting couples therapy.

The general structure used in brief work with couples is fairly consis-tent across brief therapists and is employed by the current approach. Ini-tial phone calls are used to determine the critical nature of the referral as well as financial and insurance issues. The first two sessions of the begin-ning phase are quite full. The therapist is performing a general psychological assessment of each member of the couple as well as forming hypotheses about the couple's dysfunctional dynamics. Simultaneously, the therapist is establishing rapport with the couple and then identifying and gaining consensus about those presenting complaints that will form the focus of treatment.

Work on the focal issues is rapidly and actively engaged. Couples therapy has a compressed middle phase that moves quickly into the end phase of treatment. As a result termination remains an issue throughout treatment. Significant progress can be made on the identified goals while other psy-chological issues of the couple may have to be set aside for possible later intervention (on their own or in later treatment). The therapist and couple usually spend time discussing the impact of termination. Within this struc-ture the brief self psychological model creates its form and process.

In contrast to other schools of brief therapy, self psychology criteria for patient selection are very broad and flexible. Self psychology has been used successfully with people who have a wide range of pathology, resources, and intelligence. It does require that after a few sessions both members of a couple be willing to talk and listen to each other and to the therapist. In addition, they need to be able to form at least the beginning of a self–selfobject relationship with the therapist. At least one member of the couple needs to be motivated for change, that is, wants the relationship to be better. While positive response to trial interpretations is a useful guideline for selection, we have found that, as treatment progresses, many couples can become motivated and more psychologically minded with some psycho-education and attuned responsiveness from the therapist.

The Underlying Brief Self Psychological Process in Couples Therapy

Overall, a reasoned way to conduct a self psychologically informed couples therapy is to provide a psychologically safe environment in which both members of the couple learn to understand their individual selfobject needs and consequently to be responsive to their partner's selfobject needs, that is, each to become an attuned selfobject for the other. However, making individuals aware of their own and their partner's selfobject needs may not be enough over time. Both partners have to be not only more accurate in their attunement and willing to acknowledge their partner's needs, but also willing to be responsive. The therapy experience needs to go further in helping the couple. This is imperative especially if working in a short period of time.

In the current model of brief self psychotherapy with couples, this challenge is addressed in three ways. First, the therapist temporarily joins the selfobject matrix that sustains each member of the couple. It is hoped that each partner will begin to internalize the needed selfobject functions that the therapist offers. With greater understanding and validation of each other's selfobject needs, the couple will be more giving and receptive to each other's responses. Second, the therapist promptly encourages them to enrich their support systems outside of therapy and enhance the quality of their self–selfobject relationships. Third, the therapist formally articulates the affective experiences and the concepts and the skills they are learning so that they can access them during and after termination. A therapeutic strategy and process has been set in motion that the partners will need to cultivate on their own.

Another way to view this is that the relationship that develops between the therapist and couple plus the attuned relationship that later develops between the partners are the key curative elements in couples therapy. In the therapy office there is a psychological field with three interacting subjectivities, that of the therapist and those of each partner. The therapist provides attuned responsiveness to each partner. It is often experienced as feeling deeply understood, which then adds to the vitality, continuity and cohesiveness of each partner's self. Major selfobject needs are identified, and the therapist responds partially to salient selfobject needs of each partner. Thus fortified, each mate learns to be aware of and accept his or her needs, learns how to discover the partner's needs, and to validate them and respond to them when appropriate.

Self psychological therapy may not be able to help all couples to stay together, especially if the partners have extremely different values and goals. Despite a new understanding of each other, some couples may feel it is too much work to try to make the relationship succeed and to maintain it. Even in these situations, if the partners can better understand and accept their own core needs and learn to respond empathically to another, they will make an easier separation from each other and an easier start of a new relationship.

CHRONOLOGY OF KEY FEATURES OF THE MODEL

The first goal is to create that psychologically safe environment for each partner in which to explore the issues, to learn about couple attunement, and to be willing to create a different couple experience for each other. Safety implies several things. Concretely it means that each member is free from the fear of physical and verbal abuse. Safety also implies that the individual will not be taken to psychological depths that can't be managed and will not be exposed to unbearable amounts of narcissistic shame and rage. This therapy is focal, active, and minimizes regression.

The therapy process is begun through the therapist's engaging in empathic listening and data gathering. A general psychological and self psychological assessment is undertaken regarding the couple. This is usually done nonverbally by the therapist in the course of beginning the therapy process. It only gets verbalized when the therapist is concerned about some pathology. During the first few sessions the focus of treatment is determined. There are many parallels to the procedure used for individual therapy. Specifically the major complaints of each partner are identified and then prioritized. The focus of treatment is on what underlies the recurring interactive pattern of the couple that leads to the most distress and destabilization.

The focal issue typically reflects some underlying perceived chronic lack of selfobject responsiveness on the part of one partner for the other, which leads to dysfunctional interactions and selfobject misattunement. The therapist suggests a guiding structure for the goals of therapy and seeks feedback from the couple on its design.

Emphasis is placed on understanding the meaning of the person's upsetting behavior, that is, the person's thoughts and feelings as well as the meaning of the partner's patterned response to them. Each partner is helped to identify when her own and her mate's inner reactions and behavior may be based on older self–selfobject failures being stirred up in current interaction. As is common in most interactions the therapist's position will be constantly oscillating. In one moment the therapist is helping the couple to identify the behavioral causes and consequences of the latest troubled interaction. In the next moment she may engage them in exploring the probable psychodynamic factors triggering the couple's tension. Connections are made between current psychodynamics of each partner and their history of selfobject relationships. Once these connections are identified most interpretations emphasize the present dynamics in the triangle of insight.

The focal complaint is reframed as being derived from a wish on the part of the partner for his mate to respond to his selfobject needs and a fear that they won't be acknowledged or responded to. Based on data about the couple's dysfunctional interactions, the therapist and the couple begin to identify this cycle: the wish for responsiveness, the fear and expectation of misattunement, and the preemptive maladaptive steps taken to address anticipated failure on the part of each mate. The partner's maladaptive behavior is redefined as the best effort on the part of the person to restore his self-esteem and self cohesion.

The couple is taught relevant basic concepts of psychology in simple everyday language. This always includes empathic listening, but may also include learning about selfobject needs, healthy interdependence, healthy and thwarted development, common negative affective states, and defenses, expectations, and links to behavior. We also look at the impact of a person's behavior on the couple's dynamics as a system.

Each partner is trained to listen and talk empathically through the therapist's modeling the new listening perspective and explaining how to do it. The partner watches the therapist listen empathically to the mate and hears the therapist respond in a mirroring and validating way. The partner also gets to hear the mate's experience from a potentially less defensive and more complete point of view. This often enables the partner to reconstruct a modified picture (schema) of the mate.

Cognitive-Behavioral Aspects Underlying the Therapeutic Process

Cognitive and behavioral elements infuse the therapy from the beginning. The therapist inwardly focuses on these elements during the initial assessment and formulation of the focal problems with the clients. Understanding the affective dimensions of the self experience of each partner as they interact is key. But it is also important to know the expectations each partner has of his self, significant others, the world at large, and how these expectations mediate behavior.

During the middle and end phases of therapy these elements become more obvious as the therapeutic tools are spelled out for the couple. For example, the therapist translates and decodes verbal and nonverbal communication from one partner to the other. Then the therapist teaches each partner how to decode and encode communications that can be understood by the mate by using empathic listening and observation.

Whenever possible the therapy is taken out of the therapist's office and into the daily lives of the couple. Reading on couples topics may be suggested. The couple may be given homework assignments to respond in different specific and concrete ways to their partners. This effort to get the partner to respond directly in a more attuned way also serves another purpose. It often leads the couple to new ways of thinking and feeling that are more adaptive.

During the middle and end phases of treatment specific techniques for knotty obstacles to progress may be employed, including techniques for working on physical intimacy, anger control, negotiation skills, and even relaxation training.

All this represents the beginning of internalization of the therapist's functions. The selfobject responsiveness received from the therapist is made explicit. The skills learned in affect regulation and greater flexibility in thinking and expectations are identified. Dysfunctional patterns of affect, cognition, and behavior are made clear as are the attuned patterns. Each partner is encouraged to obtain selfobject responsiveness from his mate and from others in the environment. Feelings about ending are explored, that is, the positive and negative feelings, expectations about the couple's future, and a strategy of how to handle future couple disjunctions are outlined.

When the referred couple is in crisis the therapist becomes even more active. The therapist maintains an empathic stance in order to understand the needs of each partner, explain those needs, and to respond to some of them. However, as the crisis factors are identified, the therapist does double duty as a traffic cop to prevent escalation, such as verbal attacks and physical abuse, and to allow productive talking. After empathically being informed about what is causing the crisis the therapist may have to give advice on what would be the most useful way for each partner to behave toward the other to bring the couple's dynamics under control. Once the crisis has abated, the more long-term dysfunctional self–selfobject interactions can be addressed.

Of course, some couples will want to stop after the crisis subsides. This attitude needs to be respected and explored by all parties. The couple and therapist may wish to identify what enabled the crisis to subside, what factors may cause it to flair up again, and how can they address it more proactively next time.

Rather than offer a completely manualized view of conducting treatment, I will present case examples of couples therapy informed by the brief self psychological model. As you will see, one big advantage of brief treatment is that it can heighten everyone's motivation to change. Therapists can make demands, give assignments, and set limits that may be more acceptable because it is only for a short time.

CASE EXAMPLE: BEGINNING COUPLES THERAPY

Session One

Given the level of anxiety I heard during the initial phone call from Paul and Sarah (introduced earlier), I planned to frame the therapy as a containing, soothing, and hopeful place for the couple and then discuss the agenda for the evening. Throughout our time together, I would silently be assessing their general and psychological functioning. Paul and Sarah, both slim and small, and in their late twenties, were casually dressed. I quickly noted that they were soft spoken, latter-day hippie types who clearly cared about each other. I observed that both were a little anxious, but they connected to each other in strong verbal and nonverbal ways. They both related fairly well to me. They made good eye contact and they spoke articulately and in a psychologically sophisticated manner, especially Sarah, although she seemed a little more guarded than Paul. Their overall mood was bright, and anxious but hopeful. Sarah had suggested couples treatment for over a year.

Immediately I went about establishing rapport with each. I asked how they both felt being here and what their expectations were of treatment. Sarah had been in counseling in high school and then for a year of individual therapy a few years ago. She had some idea of what it would be like but wasn't sure how it would feel to have someone else present, that is, Paul.

She felt the couple had problems but that they had a good foundation, so she assumed it could be a short-term process—12 sessions plus.

Paul concurred about his perception of the relationship but wasn't clear about the length of therapy. A close cousin had suggested treatment to him as an adolescent, but he resented it and felt he could handle his problems himself. Sensing Paul was burdened by some archaic grandiosity and partly as a way to assess his openness to explore, I offered a trial interpretation: I inquired if he might not feel he should have been able to fix all their couple problems either alone or with Sarah. Paul was receptive to my comment. He felt for a year or so that he did, but since their attempts led to roadblocks he now felt fairly comfortable with this approach. Given the goals for the evening and their obvious normal functioning, I postponed inquiring about their reasons for their prior treatment involvement.

My next goal was to obtain their presenting complaints and to train them in empathic listening. I asked both what brought them to my office. I quickly requested that they begin to talk here in a particular way to promote each really hearing the other and reduce provocations, that is, to speak only about how they experienced or felt, to use "I" statements. Each partner was to be allowed to convey his concerns without debate from the other. The other partner would then be able to ask clarifying questions and express her response to what she had heard. They continued to be cooperative and comprehended my suggestions quickly.

Sarah had a few complaints that she enumerated in a rapid, matter-of-fact way: (1) She felt that they had "problems in intimacy and communication." When Paul tried to talk with her and ask questions, he did it in a way that felt abrasive. "Paul doesn't listen to me." That would make her close up because she didn't "feel safe with him." (2) Sarah also didn't like the way Paul related to their friends. Sometimes he would be friendly to them, but at others times he would cut them off.

As she talked she realized that perhaps her resentment of his cutting off of friends happened when she felt they were disconnected as a couple. I attempted a first trial interpretation with Sarah by suggesting that perhaps her feelings about being disconnected from him were upsetting and got displaced onto his behavior with friends. She seemed to feel understood by my comment, that we were working together on this. I was also concerned that I would ask questions in a way that would enable Sarah to feel heard and understood. I began to formulate the idea that Sarah needed Paul to communicate in a highly attuned way. I briefly defined this important concept to them.

After Sarah identified her presenting complaints, Paul was asked what problems he identified. In a soft-spoken, measured way, he indicated that he liked to probe Sarah on issues that were important to her. He wanted to be able to ask challenging as well as supportive questions. Whenever he did, she claimed she didn't feel safe, he said, and then he felt censored. He would then begin to feel that they couldn't talk about anything important in the relationship or it would be threatened. He was very disappointed that she didn't feel she had a bedrock of a relationship to act from, to trust, even in conflict.

As an example, they believed that the most common area they fought about was her medical career, which preoccupied the couple a great deal. Paul and Sarah started dating about three years ago and moved in together after a year. Both had been interested in the medical field but she went further in it. Paul admitted that he had ambivalent feelings about her going to medical school and expressed it in frequent joking about it.

Going back to the original topic, Paul indicated that as he thought more about it he began to realize that he got angry when Sarah rebuffed him and withdrew. It reminded him of how he disliked that his mother used to storm off in a fight with him. In a trial transference interpretation, I suggested that that early experience with his mother may get reactivated with Sarah. Sarah added that paradoxically, when she withdraws, his response is to become more tender and attentive, even though he's reporting feeling angry inside. Slowly, Paul nonverbally agreed, and then said he just realized that because his parents were divorced, he didn't want a relationship like theirs. He wanted to stay connected to Sarah despite their conflicts.

I asked for Sarah's reactions to what Paul said. I did this routinely with each partner after the other partner spoke for a time. Sarah felt that when Paul was "unattuned" to her she would go back to "square one" in terms of trusting him. She rapidly added in a low voice that she didn't believe that any man could take care of her emotionally. She then realized that this attitude probably came from her early experiences with her detached father. She also described her mother as anxious and overly involved with her. I suggested that as a result she may not have experienced either parent as truly attuned to her, so that made relating to Paul even more complex. She agreed. I was pleased and surprised that the therapeutic alliance seemed quite good with both partners.

I now concentrated on bringing the session to a close. As part of that process I asked if I had overlooked any important issues. Sarah added a third problem: she felt that they got along very well but were like an old married couple. They were too routinized and there was not enough passion and sexuality. Sarah guessed that it would be too scary for both of them to express so many feelings to each other. Paul disagreed about it being scary. He was comfortable with the level of intensity but wanted their intimacy to be less mechanical. They had an agreement of monogamy. There was no substance dependency or major illness with which the couple had to contend.

" So Doc," Paul asked, "were we right to come here and can anything be done about our problems?" I responded that I felt their problems were quite appropriate for couples treatment and that a short-term approach did seem very doable. I indicated that I would integrate what was said in the session and at the next session I would give my assessment of their problems, the best way to help, and the time frame. I indicated that I would be interested in hearing their reactions to this session next week, too.

After the session I continued to formulate some provisional focal issues and treatment goals in consultation with a colleague skilled in brief therapy. I was concerned about not being seduced by their intellectual brightness and confusing it for psychological understanding. Therefore, I determined to keep the content of my interventions on as clear and simple a level as possible and help them to integrate their thoughts with their feelings and behaviors.

For Sarah, the lack of being understood and responded to in a precise way by Paul fed into her feeling she was chronically uncared for and was reexperiencing possible de-idealization of an important selfobject. She objected to his style of connecting to people, which she experienced as assertive, feisty, and "cognitive." When Paul experienced Sarah's angry withdrawal, he would get panicked and frustrated. But because of his possible fear of losing this important selfobject twin and his difficulty in getting in touch with his feelings, he tended to cover over the blows to his self-esteem and feelings of helplessness and resultant anger so as to prevent a breach with Sarah.

Both had intense, vunerable feelings that needed to be accepted and expressed better. I also wondered about the possibility of unacknowledged competitiveness between them, especially in the career arena. Both seemed to strongly need to feel understood and mirrored by a therapist whom they could also idealize.

They were good candidates for short-term therapy. They were already providing some selfobject functions for each other, but their breaches were eroding their relationship at a time when Sarah was becoming more successful careerwise. Given the circumscribed nature of their complaints, their good level of psychological functioning, their psychological mindedness, their degree of motivation, and most important, their ability to form a working relationship with the therapist, we were fairly optimistic about addressing their focal issues.

Their difficulties were manifested in their problems of discussing Sarah's medical school career and in feeling close and spontaneous. Given their goals I estimated an outside length of fifteen sessions and that we would reevaluate at seven sessions.

The treatment approach would be to teach them to listen and talk to each other in an empathic way and learn to respond in a more attuned way. They would be taught to discuss and work on resolving differences in an empathic way, and later they would be encouraged to seek out other selfobjects in their environment to enrich their couple world. I would also be looking at how historic patterns were affecting how they expected to hear each other, how they actually heard each other, and how they then responded to each other. The treatment would help them identify when these old patterns were interfering.

I would flesh out this formulation, indicating which things were going to be focused on and which were longer-term issues. Those issues that were not made goals for the treatment would be identified to them as potential problem areas to be monitored and dealt with on their own. That would lead into talking about possible sequential, short-term treatment.

Session Two

In my mind the goals of session two were to get their reactions to their first couples therapy encounter, and to give them my formulation of their difficulties, the treatment plan, and the time frame. We would also begin to focus on the main issues while developing a therapeutic alliance.

Paul's reaction to the first meeting was positive. They both talked a lot about it right afterward. He felt I was quick to identify what was troubling them, I understood them, and I was able to ask probing questions that drew out of him important links, especially between him and his mother. He didn't remember any negative responses but he laughed and indicated maybe he had repressed them. I took the opportunity to encourage all feedback from them, and that it was especially important to hear of their negative reactions.

Sarah's reaction was also positive. She reported some strangeness in talking about Paul in his presence. She also had some discomfort in allowing him to talk without interrupting him to explain herself. Paul added that he felt okay about waiting his turn in the session and, in fact, got the last word in the session, which he said he liked to do.

I shared my impressions about Sarah's and Paul's presenting complaints, using self psychological explanations of the dynamics and such concepts as mirroring, attunement, reactions of deflation, and the transferential links. I suggested that their focal issue related to their difficulty in communicating their needs to one another. I began discussing in general what they needed to learn. The first thing was to listen to each other empathically. I had to define and give examples of this. Paul admitted that he didn't listen empathically when Sarah was talking and realized he was trying to get her to see his point of view, that is, to put his head on her shoulders. I commented that Paul was certainly entitled to be heard but not when the expressed goal was for him to listen to Sarah, and the same rule was applied to Sarah. The second issue was to identify what each wanted inside so as to be able to communicate it to the other. Third, empathic listening would enable the couple to express deeper issues more safely. I defined these as process issues.

I also identified hot spots or content issues such as Sarah's career. She felt her career was just symptomatic of an underlying issue. Paul agreed that it was their daily interactions that were problematic in terms of being unable to discuss things. I agreed that their daily tendency to misattunement of each other's selfobject needs was more important to work on than the career issue at this time.

I indicated that there were historical factors, baggage from their families, that altered how they heard, reacted to, and recalled what they experienced with their partner. There might be some sex role differences at play as well in how they communicated. I then explained the concept of selfobject transferences in lay terms. A later goal of treatment would be to help them identify when their historical issues were interfering. I added that once they learned how to express themselves to each other, they might then need to learn how to negotiate differences.

I then brought up the suggested brief length of treatment. When I solicited their reactions, both indicated they felt I had heard them and agreed with the approach. Sarah then had some anxious concerns that this treatment would be too structured and rigid. What if she wanted to bring up something new? Paul seemed comfortable and liked the structure and felt we could incorporate new issues along the way.

I interpreted her anxiety to both of them as an understandable concern that the therapist would not address all the important issues. I responded by explaining that I was starting out more structured but would be less so once treatment evolved. If new issues came up we could choose to work on them at the time, or monitor them, and, if necessary, work on them after this treatment experience was over. I said, "The goal is not to be as short as possible but to be as responsive as possible to your goals within the time frame given." In addition, I conveyed my belief that this short-term therapy would provide them with an experience and set of skills that could continue to have a therapeutic impact after the sessions were over.

Next, I suggested we explore Sarah's career issues a little before relegating them to the back burner. Sarah was in her last year of medical school and was unable to get a good residency. She was looking for one in cardiology. This field of medicine she perceived as very competitive and jobs were hard to get, so it was easy for her to feel inadequate. Paul greatly admired her abilities but felt she didn't show them off so that others could appreciate them.

The ongoing problem has been that when Sarah came home from a difficult interview, she always assessed that she did not do well and felt deflated and somewhat despairing. Paul instantly would want to debrief and coach her while the interview was fresh. Sarah interjected, "But I'll only want to be taken care of because I feel like garbage and I want to be told I'm okay, but Paul always wants to deal with it now." Sarah was unable to effectively convey what she wanted Paul to provide. In a vulnerable state, she withdrew and Paul's comments would make her want to withdraw further, as she felt unheard and unsafe. She added that she felt some pressure from him and his family in the job arena, too.

Here I was doing what looked like parallel self psychological therapy with each individual. However, I was gathering data and providing a role model of empathic listening for both partners until they could provide that for each other in session.

Paul sadly agreed with Sarah's perception of the career dynamic between them. He indicated that she was more detached in describing it here in session. Paul explained how frustrating an experience it was for him that she was upset, that she wouldn't talk about it to him and allow him to help. If he forced it she'd get enraged. Paul claimed that when he tried to be supportive she didn't respond. Sarah nonverbally indicated that what he meant by supportive was not so to her. He felt that if he indeed waited until later to talk she would stonewall his efforts.

I asked Sarah how she experienced Paul's effort to be supportive and helpful. She described what a negative experience it was for her. Then I asked Paul how he felt when he saw Sarah upset. He replied that he felt terrible and wanted to make it so she didn't come home upset, since it was in his interest, too. Paul went on to say that he saw himself as very confident in his public life, but not so in his private life. He saw Sarah professionally as more accomplished than he was, but her greater success didn't show. It was clear that in some way he idealized her.

Paul sarcastically admitted he was not good at being a fuzzy, warm, supportive person to Sarah and that he preferred to assist by helping her to change. Paul then became concerned about what he revealed and anxiously wanted feedback regarding her reaction.

Sarah seemed agitated but didn't voice it. Instead, she defined what she meant by support. She wanted a lot of emotional support and a little coaching before an interview and maybe some debriefing after, at a time when she had calmed down from the interview. I interpreted that to mean that when she was first reacting she wanted soothing and boosting of her self-esteem and problem solving much later.

I observed Paul's need to problem solve and avoid feelings. I suggested that their different approach to handling their partner's upset was also a common disjunction between men and women. I described how each might feel inside when upset about the job interview. This enabled Paul to say that he feared if he was too supportive and acknowledged her feelings, it would make matters worse with Sarah and reinforce the problem.

Coming to the end of the session I suggested an experiment. After her next job interview they should have Paul try to stay with Sarah's reactions and then suggest later that they debrief at an acceptable time to her. Let's see if when Sarah is more responded to in the moment, she can be more responsive to his trying to help. Paul agreed to this but felt he had already tried it but it failed. He admitted maybe he didn't do it in the way that I suggested.

Paul then voiced objection to my assuming he saw job hunting as a problem-solving game. I briefly explored his reactions of feeling devalued. Paul added that he came from a family of problem solvers, which strongly contributed to his style. I thanked him for helping me appreciate his style more and suggested that we should pursue these family links next week.

Third Session

The third session's material centered on the family history of each partner. Not only did it enable me to make more accurate and attuned interventions but it helped both partners to understand and organize better the context of the other's responses as well as their own.

Sarah revealed that her beloved father was a depressed alcoholic who would withdraw for long periods while her mother would overanxiously try to control and provide everything. Paul had a bipolar-disordered mother who would threaten suicide, beg for help, and then become enraged with Paul for trying to help. Closeness in his family only came in the form of intellectual parrying about politics with his sister and estranged father.

Remaining Sessions

The remaining sessions followed a similar structure. First we would hear an update on how the couple fared during the week and how they experienced their latest home assignment. We would either pick up the threads of an incident that was a manifestation of the focal issue or take up a new one. As sessions progressed their tempo increased with more aspects of the focal issue being addressed, and more emphasis on enlarging their selfobject milieu as termination time was approaching. I was as active as at the beginning but facilitated the couple's tackling more aspects of their breaches on their own. In addition, I assisted them in developing their physical intimacy through specific sexual exercises as well as through psychodynamic exploration.

MIDDLE PHASE OF COUPLES THERAPY

Some issues and signposts to look for in the middle phase are awareness that the work of the middle and end phases overlap. There should be a strong working alliance between couple and therapist. There should be progress on the focal goals. Each mate needs to become more of a selfobject for the other, and the couple needs to develop more resources and support in their environment. Working through is going on along with discussion of termination.

The selfobject transferences from couple to therapist may change in intensity and form (for example from idealizing to mirroring to twinship).

The therapeutic transferences are used to illuminate other transferential reactions but probably won't be fully resolved. The therapist needs to be aware of her countertransference in terms of issues around separation and the need for completion.

As from the beginning, the emphasis is on taking the work in sessions out and applying it to their daily lives. This keeps the goals of treatment and ending always present and also diffuses the dependency on the therapy transference.

Elliot and Madeleine: The Middle Phase

This case was chosen to demonstrate the salient features of this approach during the middle phase, which included self psychological components and cognitive-behavioral educative aspects.

Elliot and Madeleine had completed ten sessions of couples work. They were white, middle class, with technical jobs. Both in their early forties, Elliot was an accountant and Madeleine was a dentist. As a couple they felt their relationship was stale and stalled. They couldn't decide on continuing to try for a baby. Madeleine felt her husband constantly annoyed her with his remote, intellectual style and lack of responsiveness to many of her desires for him to help her at home. Elliot couldn't stand her perceived dependencies, angry outbursts, and opinionated attitudes. He would be damned if he would have a child with a woman like this. In response, Madeleine withheld sex and affection. Elliot would then withhold his support of her and mirroring. He resorted to nightly drinking to deal with his lack of intimacy in the relationship. He often forgot the nights they needed to try to conceive.

Madeleine came from a family in which her mother was bombastic and unattuned, and her father was friendly, self-destructive, and sickly. Madeleine took care of her chronically ill father, who died at an early age. Elliot came from a controlling but erratically involved father and a loving but invisible and weak mother. Madeleine had been in individual therapy for many years that ended abruptly when her therapist died in a plane crash. Elliot had gone to therapy for a few sessions years ago to explore his struggles about commitments.

The couple had learned the elements of listening empathically and of affirming the validity of each other's reality. As a result they could sustain discussions of their differences and communicate when each felt hurt by the other. They were now able to express their anxiety and disappointment over lack of responsiveness from their mate before it turned into rage or some passive-aggressive maneuver. However, they still had difficulty in accessing and voicing what they wanted from each other.

Now they were about to come to the end of the first round of sessions, and they had planned to reassess the future of their couples therapy. Together, we articulated the gains made. They then discussed the appropriateness of further therapy regarding the couple's conflicting reactions to Elliot's anticipated career moves into academic, poorer salaried work, the lack of resolution about having a baby, and the husband's ambivalence about staying in a marriage that was so dissatisfying in affection and sex. Inwardly I felt more sessions would make sense, although they could resume at a later time.

Madeleine instantly wanted to set up another series of sessions and tossed the couple's date book to Elliot. He indicated that he might want to come less frequently, and couldn't they talk about it? As I was about to explore what he and she wanted, Madeleine twisted her body around and became flushed. Elliot asked what was the matter. Trying to control herself she blurted out, "You're always so controlling," and he stiffened and responded, "Me, what about you?"

They turned to me and asked, "Who was the one being unreasonable and controlling?" I knew I had a good relationship to both and broke the tension with a little laugh. "Madeleine, it's hard for me to simply call Elliot controlling this time when you threw him the date book and asked him to record the dates you wanted." We all laughed and then I continued, "But clearly setting up more appointments and ending therapy has particular meaning for both of you." I was validating their respective subjective reactions. "Each of you felt your concerns were overlooked by the other. Now you're both feeling alienated from one another instead of starting to work on one of your common goals. So what do you do when you run into trouble? Go back to the basics by looking at what the appointment setting meant for each of you."

Madeleine replied, "Well, Elliot, you're changing the pace of the therapy sessions without consulting me." Elliot responded, "I only wanted to entertain the idea, but now I don't think it is a good idea to come every other week, given what just happened. We can move on now if you're ready." Madeleine sat stiffly, averting eye contact with her husband.

As he resumed discussion of an issue raised last week, Elliot looked bothered and puzzled. He turned to me for an explanation of what was happening. In previous sessions I had helped decode the partners' upset communication as a way of role modeling empathic listening. Now I wanted Elliot himself to carry on some of this work.

I turned to Madeleine and said, "This may seem a little unlike our typical session but I want to give you both a little tip on how to understand your partner's communication by focusing on you, okay?" She nodded her assent. "Elliot, first take a look at Madeleine's nonverbal behavior. What do you see?" He slowly indicated that she was flushed, turned away from him, and was drumming her fingers on her leg. "So, what does that suggest to you?" I asked, prodding him further. "She seems angry but about what?" I suggested, "The last issue discussed was a likely candidate. Maybe it wasn't finished for her as it is for you. Let's ask."

Elliot asked with some bewilderment, "Are you still upset about the appointments?" Madeleine said, "Of course!" Rather than let their anger cycle into something more intense, I resumed my parallel interactions to provide some attunement to each and aid each in understanding the other so that they could reconnect. "Madeleine, it sounds like Elliot's talking about cutting back on sessions really upset you. I'm wondering if it felt like you were really undermined?" Madeleine added, "These sessions mean a lot to me. I felt like he was planning to abandon the couple therapy and me." "Elliot, can you tell Madeleine about your feelings about scheduling sessions next month and raising the idea of coming less often?" Elliot, shaken by Madeleine's concern, replied softly, "I'm not sure, but I know I'm worried about starting my new job. It's going to entail longer hours and I'm worried about being exhausted and not doing well in this new area." Madeleine seemed to relax hearing this.

I was inwardly a little confused and anxious at the perceived regression I saw in the couple's dynamics and questioned if the couple therapy should be made much longer term. At this point I could have focused on Elliot's job and career concerns previously identified, such as his possible fear of success, fear of selling out to the establishment, or fear of being overburdened. I chose to deepen the couple's understanding of the current interaction by linking their reactions to anticipated selfobject failures such as occurred in their past. This was based on their discussing their history of self–selfobject relationships in earlier sessions.

I returned to Madeleine and suggested that perhaps her reaction was strong because it stirred up similar past events with her parents. Eagerly, she explained that she could never count on her father's sustaining an interest in her concerns, and her mother always made her feel like an infant for having those needs to begin with. She anticipated in a similar way that her husband would pull out of trying to make the marriage work and belittle her for wanting any assistance. She described how with that expectation of malattunement she had reacted with intense anger and then devaluation of and withdrawal from Elliot.

Elliot looked more understandingly at his wife and nodded his head in new comprehension of her reactions. He went on to explain that when he would meet Madeleine's anger and devaluation of him it would stir up memories of not being able to get through to his stormy, self-absorbed father. He resented and became deflated over his father's plans for him, which involved having to physically and mentally exhaust himself without any acknowledgment of the cost to him from his father. He would resist his father's efforts, yet feel defeated inside. He would turn to his mother for soothing. In this current situation he could not turn to Madeleine because she had withdrawn.

The session ended at this point with each partner seeming tired but pleased to have felt better understood and fortified with better skills with which to understand the other. However, I felt a little uneasy about the wife's inability to express herself more directly and her reacting to the anticipated "abandonment" by her husband. I also felt anxious over the husband's poor skill at "reading" his wife's needs and her psychological state. It evoked in me reactions of concern for the clients, and guilt and anxiety over not doing a good enough job.

Ultimately the couple decided to renew the agreement for ten more sessions. They were able to identify their own and their partner's selfobject needs more consistently. They were more consistently able to validate those needs and respond to them. I was able to recede more and more into the background to witness and fine-tune how the couple worked on the issues between themselves. Armed with the skills they learned, the empathic experience they had in treatment, and the self-help book on saving marriages recommended to them at the beginning, they optimistically ended treatment.

END PHASE OF COUPLES THERAPY

The structure for ending brief couples therapy is very similar to that for brief individual therapy. To review: the therapist and couple need to agree that the priority focal goals have been met. The couple should be better able to recognize their own and their partner's selfobject needs and move to a more attuned state with each other. Enriched selfobject, environmental supports should be in place.

The couple will now have some tools with which to continue under-standing their particular couple dynamics and to continue working on the issues. This phase involves a consolidation of the skills they have learned with which to work through lack of attunement to each other and restore it. It also includes being able to recognize signs of self deflation, deple-tion, and fragmentation, as well as negative defensive responses that affect the couple.

As the focal goals are reached, the therapist "celebrates" the event with the couple while making reference to the ending of treatment. The couple's feelings and concerns about ending need to be discussed. Those termina-tion issues related to separation anxiety should be looked at in terms of the triangle of transference (between the patient and therapist and the patient–parent selfobject relationships). As in individual therapy, the date for termination is decided around some time of natural ending or gradua-tion for the couple, whenever that is possible.

Structure of the Termination

It is often useful, especially in couples treatment, to phase out the treat-ment by spreading out the last third of the sessions with increasing time intervals in order to give the couple a chance to put into action what they've learned and then come back and fine-tune their skills.

The couple is advised that they might have some turbulence even as they continue to work on their relationship and to wait a few months to see if they can work on the issues together. If they can't resolve the issues, the therapist needs to reevaluate the therapy approach. Consider setting up a new contract to work on the new goal or, if more appropriate, refer to individual treatment.

Down the road clients may face new developmental challenges or have new isolated crises. In that case the couple can be made aware of the op-tion of coming in for a few sessions to work on some particular issue and to tune up their couples skills and understanding.

Negative Couple Reactions to Termination

Clients may have negative reactions to ending couples therapy similar to those of people in individual therapy. Chapter 5 addressed the possible negative reactions to ending on the part of the client as well as the thera-pist. However, my experience is that negative reactions of couples may be less intense. Often self psychologically oriented therapy at least helps the partners to start to find their voice and validates their right to be heard and to obtain response from others. This enables them to feel they are entitled to reach out to others. And often the couple feels a generalized, more hopeful feeling about their relationship even if particular issues haven't been fully resolved. After the therapy is over they often still have each other, so that the feelings of separation and abandonment are alleviated. In fact, the separation from therapy may bind the couple closer.

Jasmine and Edward: The End Phase

This case is offered to demonstrate how sometimes even seasoned thera- pists have to wing it. It is also an example of how the therapist's own per- fectionism may have led to confusion within the therapist about whether the focal goals had been reached, so that when termination occurred the couple was pleased but the therapist felt the treatment was incomplete. The case, which lasted six sessions, made itself clear only in the final, termina- tion session. It may also reflect a trend in couples referrals where the pair could only loosely be defined as a couple and yet they sought help.

Jasmine was a 26-year-old lawyer of Asiatic extraction, while Edward was a 29-year-old American Yankee. She looked and acted very business- like, and looked her stated age. He was casual, hippie, grungy, and seemed younger than his stated age. Over the phone, and with great ambivalence, she had requested they meet for a few sessions to help them get over a rough phase of their relationship. She didn't want to elaborate over the phone.

During these first three sessions Jasmine was alternatively tense, angry, and then tearful, while Edward seemed more deflated, dreamily withdrawn, and philosophical about the couple's struggles. During this time I never got to identify what phase of relationship they needed help with because I ended up putting out fires instead.

Between the short time Jasmine had called and they came to my office, a long visit from Edward's ex-girlfriend was about to severely destabilize the relationship. It made sense to respond to their request that we make the new priority the impact of this visit on their relationship. I assumed this event was another stress on a vulnerable relationship and working on it would lead to the same focal issue. However, the two clients were polar- ized from each other and not willing to work much to fix things. They could not hear each other's concerns or needs.

After orienting them to both empathic listening and to eliminating debates, I explored with each what it subjectively meant for this other woman to visit. I also got some background on the history of their early self–selfobject relationships to understand better the context of their needs and concerns.

Jasmine experienced Edward as too concerned and solicitous of his ex-girlfriend. Jasmine had a history of betrayal and abandonment by her father and recent boyfriends. She felt angry and unseen by Edward.

Edward felt frustrated because he knew he loved Jasmine and was unable to reassure her. However, he resented her curtailing his socializing. He was also feeling that he couldn't help Jasmine with all of her psychological wounds.

I believed that this crisis was particularly thorny because they were in the process of trying to create more separateness and autonomy in their relationship and were having a very difficult time being physically separate. They loved each other but both felt they weren't ready for a commitment. Both wanted to grow and felt they needed to be on their own to do so. They indicated that this actually was why they originally came for help but now this crisis made their efforts at separation harder. I did question whether this referral was more appropriate for individual therapy, but Jasmine was unable to successfully work on this issue in her individual therapy and Edward didn't believe in therapy for himself.

In working on the ex-girlfriend crisis we focused on enhancing their understanding of each other's needs and on developing some negotiation skills. They were able to resolve how they would handle the woman's visit both individually and as a couple. The crisis resolved to their great relief in three sessions.

I continued to try to clarify what was the true focus of treatment. Was the crisis the focus of this brief treatment or was it the underlying conflicts about closeness and separation that they couldn't approach? Their delimiting their treatment added confirmation to this latter issue. In addition, when I would start to probe for more details from one partner about psychological dynamics or history of selfobject relationships, the other would interrupt and deflect the exploration like a tag team.

Jasmine said that she was conflicted about trusting people enough to allow herself to be close and vulnerable in a sustained way. She may have picked someone who had the same issue. Edward revealed that he thought therapy was good for others but didn't feel he needed it. He added that after his mother went into therapy, she had an affair and divorced his father and had maintained little contact with the family thereafter. He felt that he had taken on a parental-facilitator role in his family. I made an observation to him that that role may be reenacted in his relationship with Jasmine as well.

Based on what I understood, I was concerned that if Edward didn't have a voice for the feelings, thoughts, and needs that he was aware of, then he would become passive-aggressive and withdraw from her out of lack of attunement. She would then become more emotional and needy as a way to stay connected to him. This dynamic would interfere with their wish for greater separateness.

When the crisis resolved, they balked at finishing out the last two of their six sessions. I explored the possibility of a premature termination. I suggested it was not unusual in a brief therapy arrangement that they might begin to feel that as the crisis was resolved why not end even earlier, what can be accomplished in just a few more sessions? I added, "Sometimes that is true and you're ready to end. But sometimes doing that is a way of protecting yourself from some unpleasantness that endings bring, such as separating. This is the very issue that you identified." Seeing some merit to this they agreed that we would work on this for two more sessions.

I could have also addressed my other hypothesis regarding Edward's lack of disclosure in session. This related to his possible identification with his wayward mother and consequent sense of guilt. He may have feared that if he went into therapy it would make him self-centered and then he would abandon a helpless loved one. Better to stay out of it and be a facilitator. However, the mandate was clearly to help the couple through couple separation issues in the time available.

The couple seemed more relaxed but less involved in treatment. In response to my inquiry, they let me know that they were doing better as a couple; there was less tension between them and they started talking about some topics that were too difficult to touch in the past. We discussed their feeling ready to end therapy and the option to return should they need to in the future.

"Anyhow," Jasmine said, "we can only plan a month at a time since Edward will probably move away by then and who knows what will come of the relationship then?" I conveyed my surprise and asked them to elaborate. They revealed that it was likely that they would live in different states since he was taking a job out of town. He admitted his silence was a result of his fear that the more they talked about this lasting separation the more he feared she would put up a wall. He would lose her love and support even before he left. Jasmine felt she was best off dealing with her anticipated loss of Edward by focusing on becoming less needful and more indepen- dent of him.

There was an urge to explore further their withholding this information as I might have done in time-unlimited therapy. But given their plan to end shortly and not delve, I felt it was more helpful to respond to their stated wishes. I touched lightly on how difficult separations could be when both of them were in the middle of trying to define their selves and lifestyles. Separation was especially complex given their expectations from their ear- lier selfobject relationships. I suggested it might even have affected how they were in therapy and their choice to end therapy now. The comments were acknowledged but not pursued.

We spent more time on how they could enhance the time they had left and how to avoid erecting impossibly high walls. They expressed surpris- ingly strong satisfaction with their therapy experience, and some anxiety about working on their own, and then therapy ended.

As a couple they seemed to have predominantly a twinship relationship, neither wanting too much closeness, constraint, or commitment. Attach- ment in the past had been to painfully unattuned people, leaving both feel- ing that their needs were excessive and that psychological abandonment was always close by.

Jasmine provided the emotional life for the couple. Edward admired her for her guts in her career. She admired him for his lofty thinking. He was a soothing, containing, safe presence in contrast to her father. My role was to express the unmentionable in ways that wouldn't overwhelm them and help them to make the ultimate separation smoothly.

When they initially asked for help in the crisis it was ostensibly to help them lead more separate lives. I was unaware that they were probably ask- ing me to help them make a final separation. Although the subject was addressed indirectly, I believe the therapy did help on two accounts, de- spite my immediate pangs of frustration and perfectionism. First, it helped identify some of the issues making the daily attempts at separateness and individuation so difficult. Second, they now had more of a structure and method of talking and listening to each other. I hoped they could use both to be more attuned to each other and to themselves as they took their next good-bye.

CHAPTER 8

DOING BRIEF PSYCHOTHERAPY UNDER MANAGED CARE

Managed care is a very provocative term that stirs anger, fear, and condemnation in many practitioners and consumers. The term *managed care* is very broad and includes a wide variety of health service systems. Many feel these systems in their current form do a poor job both in terms of servicing the health needs of the consumer and saving money in the long run. For these and other reasons it is not clear whether these systems will survive much into the future. Why, then, deal with managed care?

However imperfect, at present, managed care organizations do represent an important referral source for clinicians, and while the latest experiments in managed care may ultimately fail, it is also likely that concerns about access to care, quality of care (including continuity), and cost will probably continue to shape health care in the future.

I am in favor of brief therapy, doing it as skillfully and sensitively as possible along with conducting time-unlimited therapy, where appropriate. Planned, brief therapy has an important role to play in this environment and in the future. My position on this issue is independent of the existence of managed care. I am quite cautious about the forms of managed care with which I affiliate and how I conduct my practice with them. The following information is offered to those who are interested in, or impelled, or challenged to become involved with managed care organizations.

American health care is reputed to be one of the most expensive in the world and getting costlier. Earlier in this book some factors were cited as

contributors to the increase in health costs. But there are other less emphasized important factors, such as the aging of the population, the demand
for higher-quality care, expensive lawsuits, and even advertising costs of
health insurance companies. The rising cost of mental health care may also
be due to factors that are not currently emphasized at all. These include
the possible increase in extensiveness and identification of psychopathology and substance abuse in the population. Managed care is one attempt
to address this situation.

The term *managed care* has evolved and been defined in a number of ways.
In its most general sense managed care refers to any health care where the
provider does not completely determine the care for the patient. Yenney
(1994) defines a managed care organization (MCO) as "an organization
that provides a system of health care services to a predefined group of
patients under a contract or on some basis different from traditional fee-
for-service and manages the services provided to that group" (p. 12). In a
traditional "fee-for-service" health care delivery system, the patient goes
to any doctor (i.e., health care provider) he chooses as long as he can pay
the fee charged by the doctor. Traditional indemnity insurance is the other
common health care delivery system. When a patient with health insurance needs medical care, the insurance company reimburses the patient for
monies paid to the doctor, or the company reimburses the doctor directly.
Aspects of traditional indemnity insurance, such as annual premiums and
copayments, may also be incorporated in a managed care plan.

Some managed care organizations simply serve as external reviewers to
keep track of the immediate expenses. Others focus on cost and quality of
care. Still others may comprehensively coordinate the client's care from
preventative intervention through chronic dysfunction.

The clinician is accountable to both the managed care organization and
the patient in terms of appropriateness of care, cost, and quality of care. It
is in these areas that the traditional clinician has not been trained to respond.

A typical managed care organization, that is, a managed fee-for-service
organization selects a panel of clinicians who are willing to provide services for a fixed, usually moderate, fee. In exchange, the therapist gets a
steady stream of referrals. Services from the providers are reimbursable up
to the time and session limits specified by the company's plan. If a plan
permits a patient to choose a therapist from outside the plan, usually the
patient pays a larger portion of the cost out-of-pocket and may also pay a
deductible.

The various kinds of managed care organizations include preferred provider organizations (PPOs), independent practice associations (IPAs), health maintenance organizations (HMOs), and point of service organizations (POSs). Managed care organizations may use an array of cost-containing systems, including case management, utilization review, treatment guidelines, and monitoring of treatment outcome. They may also have the provider of service share the financial risk in some kind of capitation arrangement. Under a capitation arrangement a provider is given one payment to cover all specified patient medical services during a specified period. At present this arrangement is most common for primary care providers. In the future this may become more common for mental health providers. Capitation puts the provider at risk of absorbing medical costs greater than the capitation payment. On the other hand, if patient costs are kept below the capitation rate then the provider can pocket the difference.

Alternatively, under managed care, a provider can have a fee-for-service arrangement, which is currently more common for mental health providers. Under this arrangement the managed care organization may regulate the number of visits and fee per visit it pays the provider in order to control expenditures. The fee-for-service arrangement does not put the provider at risk for uncompensated expenses but also offers no financial rewards for provider efficiency.

Under some circumstances a capitated managed care arrangement may offer greater autonomy to the mental health provider. Within a capitated arrangement the clinician may have more control over deciding who needs care, the kind of care, and the amount of care he provides to each patient.

Managed care and the form of its organization are continuing to change as competition affects the health care industry. However, managed care has been around for quite a while even though many of us in mental health have not been touched by it.

AN HISTORICAL PERSPECTIVE

According to Goodman and colleagues (1992), methods of systematizing the practice of health care were known as far back as the Babylonians. Efforts at accountability emphasized the practitioner's own sense of ethics and professionalism. Twenty centuries later, the American College of Surgeons was formed as an accrediting body in 1913 to develop standards for medical education and professional behavior. This was ultimately succeeded by the Joint Commission on Accreditation of Health Care Organizations (JCAHO). By 1965 both individual practitioners and institutions were accountable for quality of care.

Amendments to the Social Security Act of 1972 led to the establishment of professional standards review organizations that further formalized and enlarged external accountability of health professionals in terms of the quality of care, cost, and appropriateness of care they provided. Judicial decisions of 1982 further opened the way to external review of practitioners and made reimbursement connected to utilization of health services. Now private payers could insist on reviewing the necessity and kind of treatment *before* payment of services.

The next phase in public accountability of the practitioner as well as the institution began with the startup of the Medicare Prospective Payment System and the concept of diagnostic-related groups (DRGs). As a result the government could decide prospectively what it was going to pay for by using the diagnosis and treatment of 475 categories of diagnoses. This did not include psychiatry and substance abuse but the concept was adapted quickly and widely.

Many health care experts feel that the next phase of accountability will involve the concept of clinical indicators. Goodman and colleagues (1992) predict that by the year 2000 the Joint Commission will be establishing standards of care specific to mental health that are linked to data on patient outcome. The health care system in its current incarnation may change drastically but the need for the therapist to be more organized and accountable and give quality care probably will remain.

GUIDELINES ON WORKING
WITH MANAGED CARE ORGANIZATIONS

Clearly this is an extremely difficult time for most therapists to practice. Our autonomy is being diminished. Our income will probably be affected. The amount of time we spend on our practice will also increase due to greater need for training or retraining, record keeping, and so on. As difficult as this reality is, it may feel even more burdensome for us because of the uncertainties during this transition and our understandable intrapsychic reactions to the myriad changes. On the other hand, it is important to acknowledge that we are behavioral scientists who conduct a business practice and we need to take steps to survive and thrive.

For some clinicians the choice may be not to join any managed care organization since membership brings so many complexities and double binds with it; the mandated, time-limited nature of treatment, modest fees, and reduced practitioner autonomy are all difficult to integrate. Greater limitations on therapist–patient confidentiality and increased legal concerns about practitioner liabilities can seem hair-raising and enraging.

However, given the domination of managed care at present, the choices may be to work with selected organizations, to develop specialty skills and services that provide referral streams independent of managed care, to gather together with other consumer and professional groups to fight to change the managed care environment, or to quit working in the field.

Our first order of business regarding these massive changes is to tend to our psyches, to identify and address our own reactions, including a changing self concept, possible rage and anxiety, mourning, resignation and perhaps some excitement over rising to the challenge and growing. Our next order of business may be for us to develop a professional posture or protocol that is best for us and our clients when dealing with managed care organizations. This will facilitate a more effective (and less psychologically destabilizing) response, for example, when we are asked to expose our work or request authorization for treatment.

When working with managed care organizations, ironically what may be helpful to us is to understand their function. MCOs have a diverse range of vested interests. In addition, there is still no agreement on what constitutes quality of care. A shift in our thinking and language may be needed in order to understand the goals of these organizations and what they will reimburse. Their goals for the consumer are to alleviate acute distress that impairs functioning, or to restore a patient to an average level of functioning. They don't address the goal of existential satisfaction or happiness in life or the goal of living up to one's potential.

Most managed care reviewers vary in the amount and kind of training that they have in our field. They have to comprehend a wide array of mental health services and make sense of the different disciplines that provide those services. Part of our job is to understand what the MCOs need from us. Communicating with them becomes not only a way to facilitate our treating the client in the way we think best but also to educate them and market our skills.

We need to communicate to MCO reviewers in a common language the clinical reasons for the particular service we want to provide the patient. It's also important to articulate the patient's progress in treatment in a way they can appreciate.

One of the ways we can develop communication is to begin using more behavioral, operational language with them. For many MCOs authorization for treatment may depend on how well we communicate patient problems, treatment, and progress in those functional ways. Here are a few resources to help learn this skill.

Goodman and colleagues (1992) have created a system for documenting and communicating with external reviewers the "necessity, appropriateness, and effectiveness of mental health care services" (p. xiv). The authors don't directly address working with HMOs and PPOs. However, they suggest a way of redirecting our focus and language in order to have preauthorization and treatment plans accepted. They outline the steps we need to take in order to develop that common language. This structure may be especially helpful to clinicians who have not had much experience with utilization review and quality assurance issues.

The authors cast the patient problems and diagnoses in terms of impairments that are described in quantifiable, behavioral words, and they systematize the severity of impairment for each problem. Next, they present a set of interventions to address the various areas of impairment categories that are also keyed to a specific level of care required for the patient. Level of care refers to the range of treatment options from inpatient care, partial hospitalization, and outpatient treatment, to intensive, reconstructive private psychotherapy and supportive outpatient therapy. Behavioral outcome objectives are specified for each impairment identified. Behavioral descriptors are then used to confirm progress toward meeting the outcome objectives.

Jongsma and Peterson (1995) have simplified this process even further into six steps to aid in creating a treatment plan for thirty-four problem constellations. Once the primary presenting problems are identified, one then chooses from a list of behavioral definitions of those same problems. Next, one chooses from a list of long-term goals and associated therapy objectives, clinical interventions, and appropriate DSM-IV diagnoses.

There are also computer software programs that guide the clinician through the treatment plan. Whatever formal system of treatment planning is used, the clinician still wants to individualize the plan as much as possible to each client's unique situation.

As a self psychologist, I start a treatment plan by assessing the health of the client in traditional psychological ways and in terms of the vitality, cohesiveness, and continuity of the client's sense of self. I then tentatively identify the focal goal of treatment. Ideas about what is most needed to be improved about my client's psychological health and the focal issue are incorporated into the overall goals for the client. I then detail the focal issue and other areas of vulnerability or breakdown of the self more specifically. Mindful that managed care is oriented to reimburse treatment that helps maintain or restore a client to basic, not optimal, functioning, I look for behavioral manifestations of the problems and give examples of them. Often what are emphasized in the report are manifestations of self dysfunction in the areas of work, family relationships, social relationships, and independent functioning. The symptom pattern presented then needs to be linked up to the most appropriate *DSM-IV* axes.

I enumerate specific interventions for the focal problems itemized. Target dates are set for each problem to be worked on. For many therapists setting a target date that commits them to work for what they perceive of as an unrealistically small, limited number of sessions can be extremely uncomfortable. This is where we need to adjust our expectations to a brief therapy model, prioritize the problems of the patient, and obtain agreement from the patient as to what can be accomplished in the span of time allotted. If the therapist makes one of the aims of the therapy to help patients use more of their resources effectively, that may help assuage some of their concerns.

Disagreements with the reviewer may still occur over the number of sessions provided. A collaborative attitude here is even more necessary. If the therapist feels that the patient needs more care than the managed care organization will provide, then the clinician needs to go through the managed care organization's appeal process completely and document each step for the sake of the patient and the therapist.

Making Your Practice Attractive to the Managed Care Organization

We need to take our work seriously as a business and as a scientific endeavor. On the business side of maintaining our practice, we need to identify the different types of MCOs out there and understand the coverage and limitations for each patient. We need to know the financial standing of an MCO. We also need to be aware of the ethical issues when working with an MCO regarding provider accountability and changes in confidentiality boundaries.

Yenney (1994) suggests several improvements that will also address managed care's concern about our providing quality assurance. One would be to track patient data, such as average length of treatment, types of patients treated, success ratios by diagnostic categories, and demographics.

Keeping detailed financial records, no matter the size of the practice, will also prove useful. This information can be used, for example, to ascertain the cost/benefits of using certain treatment approaches, as well as to compare cost/benefits of working with one MCO over another. This information may also be conveyed to an MCO to market your superior cost efficiency in treating their clients over another therapist or group practice.

Another important improvement would be to use a client satisfaction survey conducted in person, by phone interview, or by written questionnaire. Almost every area of consumer service in our economy will soon be expected to demonstrate consumer satisfaction with the service rendered. It would be useful for the information to be organized in a database that could produce descriptive or quantifiable material, and be doable for the practitioner. Adding a computer system to your practice is essential at this point.

Assessment of Treatment Outcome

Another contribution we can make to the field, and the biggest change for most practitioners, would be to use standardized (test-based) psychological assessment in our practices. That contribution is one we can make on behalf of our current and future clients and on behalf of our mental health profession in order to ensure its future.

Currently, outcome research on mental health services in the outpatient and private practice sectors is still in its infancy. There are a multitude of factors that need to be considered in the assessment, such as therapeutic orientation, variety of interventions, variety of settings, and differential difficulty in working with specific types of clients. No one set of standards or psychological battery has been accepted to assess how successful a regime of therapy has been. In addition, many researchers (Russell 1994) point out that current methods of research may be inadequate and or even misleading in assessing psychotherapy. They believe that research needs to "adopt more complex and realistic conceptual models of the psychotherapy process" (p. 30).

In addition, assessment of the outcome of therapy may be viewed differently by the patient and therapist than by the MCO. The patient and therapist are understandably more interested in the health of the patient and in gaining information that will help the clinician make informed decisions. The MCO may be more interested in outcome assessment data related to quality of care issues such as number of sessions, and relapse and recidivism rates. Despite the complexities, it is essential that we practitioners begin the process of consistent, formal assessment and make our contribution.

Assessment may include using brief instruments to identify patient problems, to determine disposition of a patient, and to measure outcome of treatment, both immediate and longer-term follow-up. Ideally, it would be more helpful to the clinician if assessment were done continuously rather than pre- and posttreatment so that we could understand the course of dysfunction and the impact of the treatment better. Schlosser (1995) suggests that it include several dimensions of illness and wellness that could be addressed during the course of treatment. Taken together these efforts also form part of our providing continuous quality of care or total quality management (Maruish 1994).

The major approaches to assessment have been to use client ratings alone or in combination with therapist ratings of client improvement. Some practitioners have developed evaluations customized to each client's problems and goals. Others use standardized instruments to assess the needs of clients with a particular constellation of problems. Still others use multidimensional instruments for all clients.

Some brief self-report measures of symptom distress in adults include the Symptom Checklist Revised (SLC-90-R) and its shorter form, the Brief Symptom Inventory (BSI) both developed by Derogatis (1983, 1992), and the Brief Psychiatric Rating Scale (BPRS), which is clinician-based. Except for the BPRS, these instruments present a brief symptom checklist that the client fills out before and after treatment. The client rates himself regarding an array of possible symptoms.

Other more focused instruments are the Beck Depression Inventory (BDI-II), the Hamilton Rating Scale for Depression (HRDS) that is rated by the clinician, the Beck Anxiety Inventory, and the State-Trait Anxiety Inventory (STAI). Some multidimensional questionnaires are the revised Minnesota Multiphasic Personality Inventory (MMPI-2), and the Millon Clinical Multiaxial Inventory-II (MCMI), which, like the BPRS, is used to diagnose different clinical populations. These comprehensive personality inventories can also identify latent strengths and weaknesses outside the patient's awareness.

Two consumer questionnaires that are being used more frequently in health care settings are the Client Satisfaction Questionnaire-8 (CSQ-8; Nguyen et al. 1983), and the Service Satisfaction Scale-30 (SSS-30; Greenfield and Attkisson 1989). The first is an eight-item short form of an original thirty-one-item questionnaire. The second is a thirty-item scale that assesses many aspects of satisfaction with health services.

I agree with Schlosser (1995) that assessment needs to be "patient-centric" and should be introduced and administered as respectfully and empathically as possible. For me this means looking for and soliciting comments on the client's experience and functioning continually throughout treatment. Introducing formal assessment is made easier if the client is prepared for it at the beginning of treatment by the clinician. The clinician should explain the need and usefulness of the process. In addition, the clinician needs to inform the client of managed care's access to the material and explore client reactions to this information. The key is to incorporate the assessment into the session as collaboratively and empathically as possible. Of course, this assumes that the clinician has already worked through his own reactions to the idea of his work possibly being evaluated in this manner.

The client's reactions to the material need to be explored, acknowledged, and understood. The therapist needs to be alert to the client's possibly experiencing the assessment as an intrusion into the therapeutic relationship or as an evaluation of the client as a whole rather than of her difficulties. In addition, Maruish (1994) points out that the clinician needs to be sensitive to how information may sometimes be revealed to the therapist and client before the client is ready to process the information.

However, I have found that if one can approach the assessment as an opportunity to know the client better as well as an opportunity to improve our methods of helping people, then often the client is cooperative and even enthusiastic. Ultimately, we need to develop methods of evaluation that are better geared to the complex, multidimensional human phenomena that we are assessing. For example, this might involve using a time series approach where evaluations of the client are done at intervals instead of at only one or two points in time. This also means extending the time for follow-ups, since therapeutic changes can sometimes take a long time to manifest themselves.

For example, I informed Marie that her managed care organization had requested she fill out the Brief Symptom Inventory at the start of her managed care treatment. After she mailed it out I asked if we could discuss her experience with it. She seemed to really like my thoroughness. When I inquired further about her good feelings she shyly indicated that it gave her a chance to talk about some symptoms that we hadn't focused on. Going over her response to the questions also gave me another view on how she perceived herself. We then explored the problem areas that the questionnaire picked up. Even if we didn't add them to the list of treatment goals directly the patient felt that I understood and cared about her.

In this chapter attempts were made to help clinicians become oriented to the managed care environment, to explain how it developed and how it operates, and to suggest specific ways of working with this imperfect system of health care should they so choose. Clinician responses to managed care have varied from positive interest, to denial, to bewilderment, to the catastrophic. New clinicians are worried about gaining access to referral streams to start up a practice, while established clinicians are worried about their referral sources drying up and their livelihoods being wiped out. Those therapists working in institutional settings fear their organizations may not survive in this competitive environment.

For both new and seasoned therapists, the reality that their training may not fit the managed care model has had traumatic consequences for their self esteem and professional identity. Learning new skills and attitudes is always daunting and is even more difficult in this setting of lower fees, less autonomy, and more paper work.

Again, the reason to reorient our therapy practice and deal with MCOs is that they are big sources of referral at present. I also believe that while not necessarily manifested in the same form as in the current MCOs, our practices will be shaped by issues of cost and quality in the future, and we need to deal with these issues.

As mental health practitioners of all disciplines come together to address the impact of managed care, it is hoped that we will take back the leadership of our profession and create ways of providing quality, cost-effective care to a greater number of people while providing for the growth of the clinician as well.

What should be done next with this developing model? This is a working model of short-term therapy that I and my supervisees have found to be helpful to our patients. The short-term and longer-term outcomes of patients treated with empathic brief psychotherapy need to be systematically assessed. Other therapists trained in this approach will have to demonstrate its usefulness and effectiveness. This approach will have to be tried out on a wide range of the population with varying diagnoses and in varying situations. I am also looking forward to applying this approach to group therapy and child therapy. It needs to be compared to the other existing brief approaches. Data from this research needs to be published so that the model can benefit from peer review.

My goal in this book has been to present a model of short-term psychotherapy that is both attuned to the psychological needs of patient and therapist and is effective. Empathic brief psychotherapy is useful for three main reasons: (1) Therapists have been doing brief work unintentionally since therapy began as a profession and usually without formal guidelines. Empathic brief psychotherapy provides therapists with a flexible structure for conducting brief therapy. (2) Current changes in the marketplace and consumer psyche are pushing therapists to provide treatment in a shorter time span. (3) Self psychology, the foundation of this approach, provides the clinician with a way of working deeply and effectively with patients in a respectful, growth-enhancing way that seems adaptable to brief treatment. Integrating cognitive and behavioral aspects of functioning into the self psychological treatment enhances its impact.

Empathic brief psychotherapy is an approach that can be useful for therapists in institutional settings as well as in private practice. It may be especially useful to therapists trained in the more traditional, psychodynamic, longer-term approaches because it enables them to incorporate much of their training and experience with this modality. The main distinguishing characteristics of this approach are: (1) its self psychological core connected to cognitive-behavior features, which allows for work to be done empathically, more comprehensively, and in a timely fashion in all three main areas of psychological function; (2) the mobilizing and curative power of the therapeutic relationship, which is brought about by the internalization of selfobject functions within the patient from the therapist; (3) working deeply in a narrow sector of the patient's personality to understand the meaning of a presenting complaint in terms of selfobject dynamics and then to address it; (4) a collaborative, active effort that empowers the patient to carry on his own work; and (5) the positioning of the patient to carry on his own work and thrive within an improved self–selfobject environment of his own creation.

❖ REFERENCES ❖

Abraham, F. D., Abraham, R. H., and Shaw, C. D. (1990). *A Visual Introduction to Dynamical Systems Theory for Psychology*. Santa Cruz, CA: Aerial.

Alexander, F. (1956). *Psychoanalysis and Psychotherapy*. New York: Norton.

Alexander, F., and French, T. M. (1946). *Psychoanalytic Therapy: Principles and Applications*. New York: Ronald.

Alpert, M. C. (1992). Accelerated empathic therapy: a new short-term dynamic psychotherapy. *International Journal of Short-Term Psychotherapy* 7:133–156.

Bacal, H. (1985). Optimal responsiveness and the therapeutic process. In *Progress in Self Psychology*, vol. 1, ed. A. Goldberg, pp. 202–227. New York: Guilford.

Baker, H. (1991). Shorter-term psychotherapy: a self psychological approach. In *Handbook of Short-term Dynamic Psychotherapy*, ed. P. Crits-Christoph and J. Barber, pp. 287–322. New York: Basic Books.

Balint, M., Ornstein, P. H., and Balint, E. (1972). *Focal Psychotherapy: An Example of Applied Psychoanalysis*. London: Tavistock.

Bandura, A. (1982). The psychology of chance encounters and life paths. *American Psychologist* 3:747–755.

Barton, S. (1994). Chaos, self organization, and psychology. *American Psychologist* 49:5–14.

Basch, M. F. (1980). *Doing Psychotherapy*. New York: Basic Books.

——— (1988). *Understanding Psychotherapy*. New York: Basic Books.

Bauer, G. P., and Kobos, J. C. (1987). *Brief Therapy*. Northvale, NJ: Jason Aronson.

Beitman, B. D. (1991). Medications during psychotherapy: case studies of the reciprocal relationship between psychotherapy process and medication use. In *Integrating Pharmacotherapy and Psychotherapy*, ed. B. D. Beitman and G. L. Klerman, pp. 21–43. Washington, DC: American Psychiatric Press.

Bellak, L., and Small, L. (1978). *Emergency Psychotherapy and Brief Psychotherapy*. New York: Grune & Stratton.

Benjamin, L. S. (1991). Brief SASB-directed reconstructive learning therapy. In *Handbook of Short-Term Dynamic Psychotherapy*, ed. P. Crits-Christoph and J. P. Barber, pp. 248–286. New York: Basic Books.

Bloom, B. L. (1981). Focused single-session therapy: initial development and evaluation. In *Forms of Brief Therapy*, ed. S. Budman, pp. 167–216. New York: Guilford.

——— (1992). *Planned Short-Term Psychotherapy: A Clinical Handbook*. Boston: Allyn and Bacon.

Breuer, J., and Freud, S. (1895). Studies on hysteria. *Standard Edition* 2:1–310.

Budman, S. H., and Gurman, A. S. (1988). *Theory and Practice of Brief Therapy*. New York: Guilford.

Butcher, J. N., and Koss, M. P. (1978). Research on brief and crisis-oriented therapies. In *Handbook of Psychotherapy and Behavior Change: An Empirical Analysis*, 2nd ed., ed. S. L. Garfield and A. E. Bergin, pp. 725–767. New York: Wiley.

Chernus, L. (1983). Focal psychotherapy and self pathology: a clinical illustration. *Clinical Social Work Journal* 11:215–227.

Consumer Reports. (1995). Mental health: Does therapy help? pp. 734–739, November.

Crits-Christoph, P., and Barber, J. P., eds. (1991). *Handbook of Short-Term Dynamic Psychotherapy*. New York: Basic Books.

Davanloo, H., ed. (1978). *Basic Principles and Techniques in Short-term Dynamic Psychotherapy*. New York: Spectrum.

Derogatis, L. R. (1983). *SCL-90-R: Administration, Scoring, and Procedures Manual II*. Baltimore: Clinical Psychometric Research.

——— (1992). *BSI: Administration, Scoring and Procedures Manual-II*. Baltimore: Clinical Psychometric Research.

Dobson, K. S., ed. (1988). *Handbook of Cognitive-Behavioral Therapies*. New York: Guilford.

Elson, M. (1986). *Self Psychology in Clinical Social Work*. New York: Norton.

Ferenczi, S. (1921). The further development of an active therapy in psychoanalysis. In *Further Contributions to the Theory and Technique of Psychoanalysis*, ed. J. Rickman. London: Hogarth, 1950.

Freud, S. (1937). Analysis terminable and interminable. *International Journal of Psycho-Analysis* 18:373–405.

Gardner, J. R. (1991). The application of self psychology to brief psychotherapy. *Psychoanalytic Psychology* 8(4):477–500.

Gleick, J. (1987). *Chaos*. New York: Penguin.

Goldberg, A. (1973). Psychotherapy of narcissistic injuries. *Archives of General Psychiatry* 28:722–726.

Goldstein, E. G. (1990). *Borderline Disorders*. New York: Guilford.

Goldstein, J. (in press). Embracing the random in the self-organizing psyche. *Nonlinear Dynamics, Psychology, and Life Science* 1(3).

Goodman, M., Brown, J., and Deitz, P. (1992). *Managing Managed Care: A Mental Health Practitioner's Guide*. Washington, DC: American Psychiatric Press.

Greenberg, J. R., and Mitchell, S. A. (1983). *Object Relations in Psychoanalytic Theory*. Cambridge, MA: Harvard University Press.

Greenfield, T. K., and Attkisson, C. C. (1989). Progress toward a multifactorial service satisfaction scale for evaluating primary care and mental health services. *Evaluation and Program Planning* 12:271–278.

Gurman, A. S. (1978). Contemporary marital therapy: A critique and comparative analysis of psychoanalytic, behavioral and system theory approaches. In *Marriage and Marital Therapy*, ed. T. J. Paolino and B. S. McCready, pp. 455–566. New York: Brunner/Mazel.

Gustafson, J. P. (1981). The complex secret of brief psychotherapy in the works of Malan and Balint. In *Forms of Brief Therapy*, ed. S. H. Budman, pp. 83–128. New York: Guilford.

——— (1984). An integration of brief dynamic psychotherapy. *American Journal of Psychiatry* 141:935–944.

Hergenhahn, B. R. (1994). Psychology's cognitive revolution. *American Psychologist* 49:816–817.

Hoglend, P., and Piper, W. E. (1995). Focal adherence in brief dynamic psychotherapy: a comparison of findings from two independent studies. *Psychotherapy* 32(4):618–628.

Horowitz, M. J. (1976). *Stress Response Syndromes*, 2nd ed. Northvale, NJ: Jason Aronson, 1986.

Howard, K. I., Kopta, S. M., Krause, M. S., and Orlinsky, D. E. (1986). The dose-effect relationship in psychotherapy. *American Psychologist* 41(2):159–164.

Hoyt, M. F. (1985). Therapist resistances to short-term dynamic psychotherapy. *Journal of the American Academy of Psychoanalysis* 13:93–112.

———, ed. (1994). *Constructive Therapies*. New York: Guilford.

Hoyt, M., and Farrell, D. (1984). Countertransference difficulties in a time-limited psychotherapy. *International Journal of Psychoanalytic Psychotherapy* 10:191–203.

Jongsma, A. E., Jr., and Peterson, L. M. (1995). *The Complete Psychotherapy Treatment Planner*. New York: Wiley.

Kohut, H. (1971). *The Analysis of the Self*. New York: International Universities Press.

———— (1977). *The Restoration of the Self*. New York: International Universities Press.

———— (1984). *How Does Analysis Cure?* Chicago: University of Chicago Press.

Lachkar, J. (1985). Narcissistic/borderline couples: theoretical implications for treatment. *Dynamic Psychotherapy* Fall/Winter 3(2):109–125.

Lazarus, L. (1982). Brief psychotherapy of narcissistic disturbances. *Psychotherapy: Theory, Research, and Practice* 19:228–236.

———— (1988). Self psychology: its application to brief psychotherapy with the elderly. *Journal of Geriatric Psychiatry* 21:109–125.

Levenson, H., and Butler, S. F. (1994). Brief dynamic individual psychotherapy. In *The American Psychiatric Press Textbook of Psychiatry*, ed. R. E. Hales, S. C. Yudofsky, and J. A. Talbott, 2nd ed., pp. 1003–1033. Washington, DC: American Psychiatric Press.

Lichtenberg, J. D., Lachmann, F. M., and Fosshage, J. L. (1992). *Self and Motivational Systems: Towards a Theory of Psychoanalytic Technique*. Hillsdale, NJ: Analytic Press.

Lowman, R. L., and Resnick, R. J., eds. (1994). *The Mental Health Professional's Guide to Managed Care*. Washington, DC: American Psychological Association.

Luborsky, L. (1984). *Principles of Psychoanalytic Psychotherapy: A Manual for Supportive-Expressive Treatment*. New York: Basic Books.

Magdoff, J. M., and Greenberg, M. (1988). *Self psychological treatment of borderline-narcissistic couples*. Paper presented at the annual meeting of the American Association of Marital and Family Therapists, New Orleans, LA, December.

Magdoff, J. M., and Seruya, B. B. (1994). *Brief self psychological treatment of the individual*. Workshop presented at the Continuing studies in self psychology of the Association of Psychoanalytic Self Psychology, New York, NY, March.

Malan, D. H. (1963). *A Study of Brief Psychotherapy*. London: Tavistock.

———— (1976). *The Frontier of Brief Psychotherapy*. New York: Plenum.

Malan, D. H., Heath, E. S., Bacal, H. A., and Balfour, F. H. G. (1975). Psychodynamic changes in untreated neurotic patients, II: apparently genuine improvements. *Archives of General Psychiatry* 32:110–126.

Mandel, D. R. (1995). Chaos theory, sensitive dependence, and the logistic equation. *American Psychologist* 2:106–107.

Mann, J. (1973). *Time-limited Psychotherapy*. Cambridge, MA: Harvard University Press.

Marmor, J. (1979). Short-term dynamic psychotherapy. *American Journal of Psychiatry* 136:149–155.

Martin, J. I. (1993). Self psychology and cognitive treatment: an integration. *Clinical Social Work Journal* 21(4):385–394.

Maruish, M. E., ed. (1994). *The Use of Psychological Testing for Treatment Planning and Outcome Assessment.* Mahwah, NJ: Lawence Erlbaum.

McGuire, W. J. (1973). The yin and yang of progress in social psychology: seven koan. *Journal of Personality and Social Psychology* 26(3):446–456.

Meichenbaum, D. (1993). Changing conceptions of cognitive behavior modification: retrospect and prospect. *Journal of Consulting and Clinical Psychology* 61(2): 202–204.

Menninger, K. (1958). *Theory of Psychoanalytic Technique.* New York: Harper.

Nguyen, T. D., Attkisson, C. C., and Stegner, B. L. (1983). Assessment of patient satisfaction: development and refinement of a service evaluation questionnaire. *Evaluation and Program Planning* 6:299–313.

Ornstein, A. (1986). "Supportive" psychotherapy: a contemporary view. *Clinical Social Work Journal* 14:14–30.

Ornstein, P., ed. (1978). *The Search for the Self,* vols. 1 and 2. New York: International Universities Press.

Ornstein, P. (1988). Multiple curative factors and processes in the psychoanalytic psychotherapies. In *How Does Treatment Help?,* ed. A. Rothstein. (Workshop series of the American Psychoanalytic Association, Monograph 4) pp. 105-126. Madison, CT: International Universities Press.

——— (1991). Why self psychology is not an object relations theory: clinical and theoretical considerations. In *Progress in Self Psychology: The Evolution of Self Psychology,* ed. A. Goldberg, 7:17–29. Hillsdale, NJ: Analytic Press.

Ornstein, P. H., and Ornstein, A. (1972). Focal psychotherapy: its potential impact on psychotherapeutic practice in medicine. *Journal of Psychiatry in Medicine* 3:311–325.

——— (1977). On the continuing evolution of psychoanalytic psychotherapy: reflections and predictions. *The Annual of Psychoanalysis* 5:329–370.

Phillips, E. L. (1985). *A Guide for Therapists and Patients to Short-term Psychotherapy.* Springfield, IL: Charles C Thomas.

Pollack, J., Winston, A., McCullough, L., et al. (1990). Brief adaptational psychotherapy. *Journal of Personality Disorders* 4:244–250.

Putnam, F. (1988). The switch process in multiple personality disorder and other state-change disorders. *Dissociation* 1:24–32.

Rachman, A. W. (1989). Ferenczi's contribution to the evolution of a self psychology framework in psychoanalysis. In *Self Psychology Comparisons and Contrasts,* ed. D. Detrick and S. Detrick, pp. 89–109. Hillsdale, NJ: Analytic Press.

Racker, H. (1968). *Transference and Countertransference*. New York: International Universities Press.

Reidbord, S. P., and Redington, D. J. (1992). Psychophysiological processes during insight oriented therapy: further investigations into nonlinear psychodynamics. *Journal of Nervous and Mental Disease* 180:649–657.

Ringstrom, P. A. (1994a). An intersubjective approach to conjoint therapy. In *Progress in Self Psychology: A Decade of Progress*, ed. A. Goldberg, 10:159–182. Hillsdale, NJ: Analytic Press.

———— (1994b). *Exploring the model scene: Finding the focus in an intersubjective approach to brief psychotherapy*. Paper presented at the meeting of the 17th Annual Conference on The Psychology of the Self, Chicago, IL, October.

Russell, R. L., ed. (1994). *Reassessing Psychotherapy Research*. New York: Guilford.

Saakvitne, K. W., and Abrahamson, D. J. (1994). The impact of managed care on the therapeutic relationship. *Psychoanalysis and Psychotherapy* 11(2):181–199.

Sampson, E. E. (1994). Sperry's cognitive revolution. *American Psychologist* 49:818–819.

Schlosser, B. (1995). Clinical outcomes assessment: a patient-centric perspective. *The Independent Practitioner* 15(3):131–133.

Schwartzman, G. (1984). Narcissistic transferences: implications for the treatment of couples. *Dynamic Psychotherapy* 2(1):5–17.

Seligman, M. E. P. (1995). The effectiveness of psychotherapy: the *Consumer Reports* study. *American Psychologist* 50(12):965–974.

Shapiro, D. A., and Shapiro, D. (1982). Meta-analysis of comparative therapy outcome studies: a replication and refinement. *Psychological Bulletin* 92:581–604.

Siddall, L. B., Haffey, N. A., and Feinman, J. A. (1988). Intermittent brief psychotherapy in an HMO setting. *American Journal of Psychotherapy* 42:96–106.

Sifneos, P. E. (1979). *Short-term Dynamic Psychotherapy: Evaluation and Technique*. New York: Plenum.

Smith, M. L., and Glass, G. V. (1977). Meta-analysis of psychotherapy outcome studies. *American Psychologist* 32:752–760.

Smith, M. L., Glass, G. V., and Miller, T. I. (1980). *The Benefits of Psychotherapy*. Baltimore: Johns Hopkins University Press.

Solomon, M. F. (1988). Self psychology and marital relationships. *International Journal of Family Psychiatry* 9(3):211–226.

———— (1989). *Narcissism and Intimacy*. New York: Norton.

Sonnefeld, S. T., Waldo, D. R., Lemieux, J. A., and McKusick, D. R. (1993). Projections of health care spending through the year 2000. *Health Care Financing Review*, Fall.

Sperry, R. W. (1993). The impact and promise of the cognitive revolution. *American Psychologist* 48:878–885.

Stern, D. N. (1985). *The Interpersonal World of the Infant*. New York: Basic Books.

Stolorow, R. D., Brandchaft, B., and Atwood, G. E. (1987). *Psychoanalytic Treatment: An Intersubjective Approach*. Hillsdale, NJ: Analytic Press.

Strupp, H. H., and Binder, J. L. (1984). *Psychotherapy in a New Key: A Guide to Time-limited Dynamic Psychotherapy*. New York: Basic Books.

Strupp, H. H., and Hadley, S. W. (1979). Specific versus nonspecific factors in psychotherapy: a controlled study of outcome. *Archives of General Psychiatry* 36:1125–1136.

Strupp, H. H., Schacht, T. E., Henry, W. P., and Binder, J. L. (1992). Jack M.: a case of premature termination. *Psychotherapy* 29(2):191–205.

Taube, C. A., Goldman, H. H., Burns, B. J., and Kessler, L. G. (1988). High users of outpatient mental health services, I: Definition and characteristics. *American Journal of Psychiatry* 145(1):19–24.

Thelen, E., and Smith, L. B. (1994). *A Dynamic Systems Approach to the Development of Cognition and Action*. Cambridge, MA.: MIT Press.

Tolpin, M. (1986). The self and its selfobjects: a different baby. In *Progress in Self Psychology*, ed. A. Goldberg, 2:115–128. New York: Guilford.

Trop, J. L. (1994). Conjoint therapy: an intersubjective approach. In *Progress in Self Psychology: A Decade of Progress*, ed. A. Goldberg, 10:147–158. Hillsdale, NJ: Analytic Press.

Ulman, R. B., and Paul, H. (1990). The addictive personality and "addictive trigger mechanisms": the self psychology of addiction and its treatment. In *Progress in Self Psychology: The Realities of Transference*, ed. A. Goldberg, 6:129–156. Hillsdale, NJ: Analytic Press.

Waldorp, M. M. (1992). *Complexity: The Emerging Science at the Edge of Order and Chaos*. New York: Simon & Schuster.

Weiss, J., Sampson, H., and the Mount Zion Psychotherapy Research Group. (1986). *The Psychoanalytic Process: Theory, Clinical Observations, and Empirical Research*. New York: Guilford.

White, M. T., and Weiner, M. B. (1986). *The Theory and Practice of Self Psychology*. New York: Brunner/Mazel.

White, R. W. (1959). Motivation reconsidered: the concept of competence. *Psychological Review* 66:292–333.

Wolf, E. F. (1988). *Treating the Self: Elements of Clinical Self Psychology*. New York: Guilford.

Yenney, S. L., and American Psychological Association Practice Directorate. (1994). *Business Strategies for a Caring Profession: A Practitioner's Guidebook*. Washington, DC: American Psychological Association.

❖INDEX❖

Abraham, F. D., 50
Abrahamson, D. J., 3, 99, 101
Adjunctive treatments, therapist/client
    issues, 102–104
Alexander, F., 29, 32, 33, 36
Alpert, M. C., 58
Attkisson, C. C., 142

Bacal, H., 24
Baker, H., 11, 16, 40, 58
Balint, M., 10, 37, 55
Bandura, A., 52
Barber, J. P., 27, 32, 40
Barton, S., 50
Basch, M. F., 61
Bauer, G. P., 29, 32, 33, 87, 88
Beck, A., 41
Beitman, B. D., 27, 103
Benjamin, L. S., 40
Bibliotherapy, brief psychotherapy
    and, 102
Binder, J. L., 39

Birth trauma, 35
Bloom, B. L., 1, 5, 27, 32, 44
Body therapy, brief psychotherapy
    and, 102
Brief psychotherapy, 27–47. *See also*
    Cognitive-behavioral therapy;
    Self psychology
    application of, 58–60
    case example, 62–64
    cognitive-behavioral therapy and,
        40–44
    cognitive-behavioral therapy and
        self psychology, 44–47
    concepts
        current, 49–55
        generally, 28–31
    couples therapy, 105–131. *See also*
        Couples brief psychotherapy
    cure and, 60–61
    described and defined, 3–6, 27–28
    development of, 1
    historical perspective on, 32–40

Brief psychotherapy (*continued*)
  individual, 65–93. *See also*
    Individual brief psychotherapy
  managed care and, 133–144. *See*
    also Managed care
  personal approach to, 7–8
  psychodynamic approaches,
    varieties among, 31–32
  self psychology and
    early integrations, 55–58
    generally, 8–10
Budman, S. H., 109
Butcher, J. N., 5
Butler, S. F., 32, 40

Chaos theory, 51, 53
Chernus, L., 56, 57
Client/therapist issues. *See* Therapist/
  client issues
Cognitive-behavioral therapy. *See also*
  Brief psychotherapy; Self
  psychology
  brief psychotherapy and, 40–44
  couples brief psychotherapy, 112–
    114
  self psychology integrated with, 44–
    47, 61–62
Confidentiality, managed care and,
  99–100
Consumer Reports, 4, 5
Cost containment, health care system,
  2–3
Countertransference, termination, 88
Couples brief psychotherapy, 105–131
  breakdown dynamics, 107–108
  case example, 114–131
    beginning phase, 114–122
    end phase, 126–131
    middle phase, 122–126

chronology in, 111–114
  overview, 105–107
  self psychology and, 109–111
Crits-Christoph, P., 27, 32, 40
Culture, self psychology and, 11–12

Davanloo, H., 29, 37, 38, 39, 58
Diagnostic and Statistical Manual of Mental
  Disorders (DSM-IV), managed care
  and, 138, 139
Dobson, K. S., 42, 44

Ellis, A., 41, 44
Elson, M., 40, 57
Empathic brief psychotherapy. *See*
  Brief psychotherapy
Empathic listening, therapeutic
  relationship, 23–24
Empathy
  self psychology and, 12
  therapeutic relationship, 23
Exercise, brief psychotherapy and,
  102
Eye movement desensitization and
  reprocessing (EMDR), brief
  psychotherapy and, 102

Facilitative responsiveness, therapeutic
  relationship, 24
Farrell, D., 95
Ferenczi, S., 32, 33, 34, 35
Flegenheimer, W., 40
French, T. M., 32, 36
Freud, S., 11, 13, 14, 15, 28, 32, 33,
  34, 51, 54

Gardner, J. R., 40, 57
Glass, G. V., 5
Gleick, J., 50

Goldberg, A., 56
Goldstein, E. G., 17
Goldstein, J., 53
Goodman, M., 135, 136, 138
Greenberg, J. R., 14
Greenberg, M., 19
Greenfield, T. K., 142
Gurman, A. S., 108, 109
Gustafson, J. P., 9, 10

Hadley, S. W., 5, 70
Health care system, 1–10
    crisis in, 2–3
    managed care and psychotherapy,
        3
    mental health profession and, 1–2
Hergenhahn, B. R., 51
Hoglend, P., 69
Horowitz, M. J., 39
Howard, K. I., 4, 6
Hoyt, M. F., 5, 43, 44, 95, 97, 98
Hypnotherapy, brief psychotherapy
    and, 102

Idealizing, selfobject relationships, 18
Individual brief psychotherapy, 65–93
    case examples, 71–86
        beginning phase, 71–80
        middle and end phases, 80–86
        termination, 88–90
    initiation of, 65–66
    self-statement assessment, 66–67
    stance in, 70–71
    termination
        countertransference reactions, 88
        identification of early termination
            clients, 70
        negative reactions to, 87–88
        steps in, 86–87

therapist/client issues, 96–104.
    See also Therapist/client issues
treatment focus establishment,
    68–70
Infancy, self psychology and, 13–15
Internalization, transmuting,
    selfobject relationships, 19

Jongsma, A. E., Jr., 138

Kobos, J. C., 29, 32, 33, 87, 88
Kohut, H., 7, 9, 11, 12, 13, 14, 15,
    16, 17, 18, 19, 20, 21, 22, 24, 41,
    54, 56, 60
Koss, M. P., 5

Lachkar, J., 106
Laikin, M., 40
Lazarus, A., 41
Lazarus, L., 56
Lazarus, R., 41
Levenson, H., 32, 40
Lichtenberg, J. D., 9, 18, 24, 58
Lowman, R. L., 3
Luborsky, L., 39

Magdoff, J. M., 7, 18, 19, 108n
Mahler, G., 33
Malan, D. H., 5, 29, 33, 36, 37, 38, 55
Managed care
    guidelines for, 136–144
    historical perspective on, 135–136
    overview, 133–135
    psychotherapy and, 3
    therapist/client issues and, 98–102
Mandel, D. R., 52
Mann, J., 36, 37
Martin, J. I., 61
Maruish, M. E., 141, 142

McCullough, L., 40
McGuire, W. J., 50
Meichenbaum, D., 41, 43
Menninger, K., 29
Mental health profession, health care
    system and, 1–2
Mirroring, selfobject relationships,
    17–18
Mitchell, S. A., 14

Narcissism, self psychology and, 13

Object relations theory, self
    psychology and, 12
Optimal frustration/optimal
    responsiveness, therapeutic
    relationship, 24–26
Ornstein, A., 14, 15, 37, 55, 56, 57
Ornstein, P., 37, 55, 56, 57
Outcomes
    brief psychotherapy, 5–6, 60–61
    managed care and, 140–144

Paul, H., 75, 76
Peterson, L. M., 138
Pharmacotherapy, brief psychotherapy
    and, 102–104
Phillips, E. L., 41, 44
Pinsker, H., 40
Piper, W. E., 69
Pollack, J., 40
Psychodynamic approaches, brief
    psychotherapy, varieties among,
    31–32
Psychotherapy, managed care and, 3
Putnam, F., 52

Rachman, A. W., 35
Racker, H., 95

Rank, O., 32, 33, 35, 37
Redington, D. J., 52
Reframing, self psychology and, 19–
    22
Reidbord, S. P., 52
Resnick, R. J., 3
Ringstrom, P. A., 67, 106, 108
Rogers, C., 12

Saakvitne, K. W., 3, 99, 101
Sampson, E. E., 51
Sampson, H., 40
Schlosser, B., 141, 142
Schwartzman, G., 106, 107
Self-help groups, brief psychotherapy
    and, 102
Selfobject relationships, self
    psychology and, 17–19
Selfobjects, self psychology and, 16–
    17
Self psychology, 11–26. See also Brief
    psychotherapy; Cognitive-
    behavioral therapy
    brief psychotherapy and, 8–10
    early integrations, 55–58
    cognitive-behavioral therapy
        integrated with, 44–47, 61–62
    concepts, 53–55
    couples brief psychotherapy and,
        109–111
    empathy and, 12
    infant research and, 13–15
    narcissism and, 13
    overview, 11–12
    self and, 15–22
        concepts, 15–16
        reframing, 19–22
        selfobject relationships, 17–19
        selfobjects, 16–17

therapeutic relationship, 22–26
  empathic listening, 23–24
  empathy, 23
  generally, 22–23
  optimal frustration to optimal
    responsiveness, 24–26
Self-statement assessment, individual
  brief psychotherapy, 66–67
Seligman, M. E. P., 5
Seruya, B. B., 18
Sexuality, self psychology and, 14
Shapiro, D., 4
Shapiro, D. A., 4
Short-term therapy. See Brief
  psychothcrapy
Siddall, L. B., 34
Sifneos, P. E., 5, 29, 36, 38
Smith, L. B., 50, 51, 52
Smith, M. L., 4, 5
Solomon, M. F., 106, 107, 108
Sonnefeld, S. T., 2
Sperry, R. W., 51
Stern, D. N., 14
Stolorow, R. D., 16, 67
Strupp, H. H., 5, 39, 70

Taube, C. A., 5
Termination
  case examples, 88–90
  countertransference reactions, 88
  couples brief psychotherapy, 127–131
  identification of early termination
    clients, 70

negative reactions to, 87–88
steps in, 86–87
Thelen, E., 50, 51, 52
Therapeutic relationship, self
  psychology, 22–26. See also
  Self psychology
Therapist/client issues, 96–104
  adjunctive treatments, 102–104
  managed care and, 98–102
  problematic reactions, 95–98
Tolpin, M., 14
Transmuting internalization,
  selfobject relationships, 19
Trop, J. L., 106
Trujillo, M., 40
Twinship, selfobject relationships,
  18

Ulman, R. B., 75, 76

Waldorp, M. M., 50, 53
Walter, B., 33
Weiss, J., 40
White, R. W., 18
Wiener, D. N., 44
Winnicott, D. W., 12
Winston, A., 40
Wolf, E. F., 11, 15, 18, 19, 20, 21
Wynter, C. E., 53

Yenney, S. L., 2, 134, 140
Yoga, brief psychotherapy and,
  102